Why I Gave Away £2.4 Million Pounds

Why I Gave Away £2.4 Million Pounds

THOMAS TUCKER

PublishingPush

Copyright © 2022 by Thomas Tucker

All rights reserved. No part of this book may be reproduced or used in any manner without written permission of the copyright owner except for the use of quotations in a book review.

FIRST EDITION

ISBN 978-1-80227-327-4 (paperback)
ISBN 978-1-80227-384-7 (hardback)
ISBN 978-1-80227-326-7 (ebook)

Published by PublishingPush.com

Typeset using Atomik ePublisher from Easypress Technologies

WHY I GAVE AWAY
£2.4 MILLION POUNDS

*This is a true story with some lessons to be learned.
I had to change some names.*

You could say it all started when I was around 3 years old; at least, that's as far back as I can remember. I recall walking round the house with a plastic bucket because I had whooping cough, and the bucket was for me to be sick into. On one Saturday night, when my Mum used to go to the Labour Club, I remember all I wanted was for her to hug me, but as I walked, crying, into the bathroom with the bucket, she lifted her leg and pushed me backwards and I fell on the floor. The contents of the bucket went all over me and she went mad. She gave me a cloth to clean it up and after that, I understood she wasn't going to hug me and that she didn't care; she just wanted to go out and spend the night getting pissed while one of the girls was looking after me.

When Christmas time came and it snowed, we all went out to play; putting socks on our hands because we didn't have any gloves. We still had a good time with the young ones in the street though, and we were left out for hours, even at night time because there were no cars on the snowy road. On Christmas Day, it was like being back in the 1940s at the time of rationing. You got a tangerine, an apple and a bag of nuts; you needed a house brick to break open the nuts, but we still had a good time. Mum always made a Christmas dinner as she paid 50p a week for the hamper beforehand, so there was a lot of food. After she'd had a few drinks, she would always let us have some of her chocolates. Looking back to when I was young, I remember that we had snow all the time in December and the summer was always very hot; you wore just a pair of shorts and pumps or trainers.

The next few months dragged and then I turned four, but you didn't get any gifts on your birthday; you got some money to get sweets – usually around ten pence, which was a lot back then. As it came up to summer, I was taken to the farm with the rest of my brothers and sisters. It was hard being the ninth child. I had six sisters and three brothers; the two older ones had got married and left leaving 8 of us at home. We used to work at the farm from 8 am until 6 pm picking peas, and when you filled your basket you got a round washer, which you put on a string around your neck, that showed the weight of the peas handed in. Sometimes, we would sneak away and try to steal as many washers as we could find to add to our own! The field was huge and full of families from all round the area where I lived, and we could have some fun with the rest of the kids from the estate. We weren't given any breakfast or dinner before we left home, so, often, Mum would send us home to make a bottle of tea. Since we didn't own a flask, we had to fill a milk bottle with the tea then when we walked back, we would have a drink and eat as many peas as we could. They also used to store apples in one of the barns on the farm, so we would lift up the corner of the corrugated iron wall and crawl in, passing the apples out through the hole, and handing them out to the people we knew. It was like having a second course for your dinner but by the time you left, you had stomach ache. To be truthful, it was child labour. If you didn't work hard, you got a slap off your mum. Even though most of your friends were there, you weren't allowed to play with them as we had to keep picking peas.

When we got home, it was the normal tea - chips and beans with bread, and you were allowed only two slices of bread, but this was something we were all used to. As soon as we'd finished our tea, the girls would wash the dishes, clean the kitchen and hoover the front room. Then we had to leave the house until 9 pm to give Mum time on her own to watch the old black and white TV we'd been given by my eldest brother. My Dad worked shifts and had two days off. He worked either 6 am–2 pm, 2 pm–10 pm or 10 pm–6 am and when he wasn't working at night, he'd go for a drink with his best mate who lived next door. We normally had to be in the house for 9 pm and then go straight to bed with nothing to eat or drink. We lived in a three-bedroom council house. I used to sleep between two of my sisters and the other two would top and tail in a single bed. My brothers had two single beds in their room and Mum and Dad had a double bed in their bedroom. We had one blanket and that was covered by a couple of long, thick army overcoats. We had only lino on the floor, no carpet, and no heating except for a coal fire downstairs, and the windows were single-paned; in the winter, the glass used to ice up on the inside of the window and we were fucking freezing.

Every morning, there'd be a rush for the bathroom for the girls. I didn't matter much, so my Mum used to spit on her hanky and wipe my face and I'd give my hair a quick brush. After that, I would walk down the street, across the ring road and get the bus on my own. It cost a penny and it got me close to school. Most of the time I would lie down under the bus seats so the conductor couldn't see me, so I could keep the penny for sweets. I'd say that most of the time it worked but some conductors had seen it done, so they would drag you out by the hair and make you pay. It was a bit embarrassing if you were trying to impress your mates and you were covered in dust from the floor of the bus, and it took ages to get the dust off your clothes.

We played out most nights with all the lads and girls from around the estate; we played in the swing park, as we called it. This place had 4 swings, a roundabout and a sliding horse, and we spent almost every night either there or on the ring road playing football. Where we lived was lovely when I was young. Everyone got on and you knew everyone in the street. When Dad was going to work at around 5 in the morning, Mum didn't usually get up. When we got up for school, my sister would get me dressed and I'd walk up the hill with her; then she would go into her school and I got the bus as it was another 3 miles to my school.

As a 4-year-old, I struggled to cope with what was happening to me, especially as I was finding it hard to go to the toilet and if I had an accident, Mum would give me a good smacking, but I tried to put it to the back of my mind; I was scared of telling anyone in case I got in trouble myself. It was just brushed under the carpet as it was hard to tell people and I was frightened of the outcome. We had a girl in our infant class at school who use to go under the desk and pull your shorts down and play with your willy, but we thought it was just the normal thing that kids did; she would put her fingers inside herself and try to get you to smell them, but again, it's only when you get older you can understand she must have been abused herself at home. I don't remember much of my time at infant school apart from having a small bottle of milk every day and that we use to be allowed to go to sleep on a mat. I couldn't control my bowels, so I kept away from the rest of the kids as I got to 5 years old, and as time went on, the problem seemed to get worse. It was shocking, and to be truthful, I would soil myself more and more often, which not only make me feel awful, but my Mum would kick the crap out of me and I mean she would belt me round the head a few times and make me take off my clothes and wash my underwear in the sink. This went on for a few months and I was at the doctor's most weeks, and she was beating me every day. My sisters would take me out to stop me from getting beaten. All of a sudden, the doctor said,

"He may need to go to hospital."

Later that day I was taken into hospital, put in the children's ward, and left on my own.

Fuck me, I hated it. The nurses were unfriendly and no one spoke to you. Every day, a teacher came in and we had lessons that were a little different from normal school, but we still did reading and writing, and loads of painting. Then every single fucking day, a nurse used to come and take a blood sample and that really hurt. As time went on, I started to run out of fingers to prick. I used to run away as soon as I saw the trolley come through the doors and I went to hide in the toilet, but she would come to get me. I would climb out of the window onto the fire escape and sit with my back against the wall so she couldn't see me. Then, when she'd left the ward, I would climb back in. However, when I had afternoon school lessons, she'd come back and get the blood then. I hated her even though she was just doing her job. There were many times when I wouldn't let them do it and the nurses would get hold of me and strap me to the bed with a big leather strap across my body and more straps on my hands and feet. It was awful. I hated the place and didn't talk to anyone. Every day I had doctors poking me and feeling my stomach and making me piss in a bottle for tests, and go to the toilet on a bedpan so it could be tested. Nothing changed. It was the same every day; I hated all of it and I didn't get many visitors – when I say that I mean they came very rarely in the afternoon, so I sat alone.

Each day, someone would come into the ward and the nurse would shout my name, put me in a wheelchair and take me to different parts of the hospital; in one place they shoved a rubber tube up my bum and filled it up with some blue liquid then took me for an X-ray. After that, they'd take me to another room to do something else, then back to the ward; this went on for months. After the X-ray, I had to stop at every toilet on the way back as I was exploding blue liquid and felt very scared. I remember one day when I wasn't well and I wanted to go home; I'd been in for about 3 months by then and my Mum had been coming twice a week, and my sisters sometimes came in the evening; I didn't get any visits in the afternoon. One afternoon, when every kid in the ward had visitors apart from me and the nurses were having a cup of tea and a chat, I walked out of the main doors and tried to find my way out of the hospital. A doctor stopped me and asked where I was going, and I said my Mum was in the hospital shop round the corner so I was going back to her. He said okay and walked off.

After that, I kept trying to hide from anyone with a uniform, but the corridor was full of people in uniforms, so I opened a door that I thought went outside and it was a big room with all the cleaning stuff and a little table with some chairs around it for the cleaners to use. They had a fridge with pop inside and there were also biscuits on the unit near the sink, so I had a drink and some biscuits then sat down for a rest. My plan was to go to sleep for a bit until it got dark, then make my way home. I got all the coats and the clothes and put them in the corner to make myself comfortable. I had no idea there was a full-scale alert out for me in the hospital and the police even came. They'd gone home and picked up my Mum. Anyway, I fell asleep and the cleaner found me later. She woke me up and asked me which ward I had come from; she was lovely, very kind and caring, and I was crying. I told her I wanted to go home and asked if she would take me, but she sat me on her knee and explained to me how things worked at the hospital and told me things would be fine soon; they needed to look at me to see what was wrong, then put it right and I could go home. At that moment, I was wishing that she was my Mum; that's not a nice thing to say but I didn't have a very good life after all. I started falling asleep again on the cleaner's knee and then a nurse came in the room and I remember the cleaner saying,

"He's ok, but just very scared." The nurse was going on about me having been missing for hours and how security was looking for me and the police had been called. The cleaner looked at her and said,

"He's frightened, that's all", and gave me a kiss.

The nurse used the telephone and told someone she'd found me in the cleaner's room and that I was okay.

Then another nurse came, picked me up, took me out to the corridor, and then put me in a wheelchair. She said that what I'd done was very naughty and she took me back to the ward. They put me into the bed, again putting the wide leather strap around my waist and strapped me down, with my hands also strapped to each side of the bed. No matter how much I tried and cried, I couldn't move. I remember seeing my Mum just walking away; she didn't even come to sit with me. It was torture. None of the nurses would talk to me and my Mum had walked off and left me, so all I could do was look up at the ceiling.

The evening visiting time came and every bed had 3 to 6 people sitting around it but I had no one; I was strapped down like a killer on Death Row. I had to give in. Even the nurses stopped talking to me, but a nice lady who was visiting a girl in the next bed kept looking at me; I smiled at her and she smiled back but we didn't speak. Then she came over and put some orange cordial in my water jug, poured some into a glass, then lifted my head and gave me a drink.

"Thank you," I said.

"It's ok, sweetheart, you'll be fine," she said.

She put some sweets at the side of my pillow and said,

"Try to get some sleep, love."

She held my hand for a bit then the nurse came over and gave me a drink that didn't taste nice at all. She asked the lady to go back to the girl and pulled the curtains round my bed so no one could see me; then I was out like a light all night. All I remember was the lady in the morning putting breakfast on my tray and it was cereal; I'd never had cereal before because Mum never ever bought any, but as I said, we didn't get breakfast at home. It was only if Mum had gone to get her hair done that my sister would make some toast, but we had to open the windows and doors so she couldn't smell it when she got back.

I was around 5–6 years old and living at home was not nice. All Mum did was shout all day and that's why you had to be out of the house. If it was raining and your friends had gone home for dinner, we were sometimes allowed in, but normally, it wasn't until after tea time. To keep out of her way, I used to hide at the bottom of our stairs where there was a cupboard with the electric and gas meters in it and I had to move a row of around 10 coat hangers, mainly for Mum and Dad's coats, to make space. He had a long mac for winter and I would get on the second step and put the mac around me so no one could see me because Mum might come to put money in the gas meter. I saw this as a safe place; just me on my own. I didn't want to go upstairs because I was scared of the upstairs; I don't know why. But when you wanted to go back outside, you would have to use the front door because if you walked past Mum in the front room, she would stop you to ask what you'd been doing upstairs. She would check your pockets then give you a smack around the head and send you outside, so to save all this, you could open the front door and try to close it quietly but even then, she would usually be there at the door shouting,

"What are you doing? What have you got? Why have you used the front door?"

"I haven't," I would say, "I just hit the door with the ball."

And she would rant on: "Get out; move away from the door. I'll shout you in later!"

It was hard work. A new lad moved in nearby and we become friends. When I went to his house, his Mum was amazing; she would make me a cup of tea and some toast. Also, he got treated like a prince. When he asked for money, she asked how much he wanted. When she got him clothes, she let him choose the colour. It was a different world. Every time he went out, she gave him a kiss! The last time I got a kiss, it was from my Auntie. She was a lovely woman; very kind and always gave you a big hug and a couple of pence for sweets.

I remember going to my Auntie's house with Mum – she didn't live far away – and she had school pictures of her children around the place. I had my picture taken at school every year as well, but Mum never bought one photo - not of any of us, come to think of it. There were no photos in our house of anyone. Also, I never had a watch because there was no way she would buy us all one. I did learn to tell the time at school but I was very envious of people with a watch, and the other thing I didn't have was football boots for sports. We used to play rugby but I had only my trainers. One afternoon when I was at school, I went into lost property and found a pair of football boots. I hid them in the bushes outside and when everyone went home, I went back and got them. I had to colour in the green stripes on each side and I did it with black spray paint that I got from my friend. They were a bit big but I used to put two pairs of thick socks on when we played sport. They did make me trip over a lot, but I kept them anyway. The black spray ended up coming off but I still liked them because they were mine.

I have to say that writing this down is making me sad; I think it's because I have my own children now and would give the world for them. I spent one year and three weeks in hospital and in all that time, my dad never came to see me. I understand now it was because he was working all the time. As I said, my Mum would come only a couple of times a week and my sisters would sometimes call in at night but most of the time I was on my own, just watching all the other visitors giving their kids colouring books and jigsaws when all I got was a vampire nurse who took blood from me every day. I use to wonder what the fuck she was doing with it all, but it went on for a long time. One Saturday, when my eldest sister was getting married, I was let out. I was picked up and dressed, then taken to the church and I posed in the wedding photos afterwards. As soon as the photos were done, I was taken back to the hospital, just after the afternoon visiting had finished. I don't even remember who took me back. I was undressed and put back into bed, then I got up for tea, and then sat watching TV. Soon after, the nurse came and took me back to my bed as it was visiting time. When I looked around, I saw the whole ward was full of visitors, with chairs around every bed apart from mine; but I'd got used to that by then. I got out of bed again and went back to watch TV but this nurse told me to get back into bed. I refused because I was watching TV, so she picked me up and took me back and out came the straps again. After leaving the hospital where I'd been for over a year, no one even said anything when I got home; it was as though I'd just nipped out to the shop. Nothing had changed, and Mum was still the same bitter old lady she'd been before. I'd had an operation at some point and something was fitted into my bowel. I had no idea when they'd done it as I was taken out of the ward a few times a week, but anyway, this seemed to fix whatever was wrong inside me at the time. After that, I could only go to the toilet twice a week and that blocked the toilet each time, and I was made to unblock it myself. Mum would say that I'd blocked it so I had to sort it out.

When I was let out of hospital, my eldest sister had moved about 3 miles away from our house and I was gutted, but I used to walk to her house on a Saturday morning. I was only 6 or 7 years old. My sister's husband was a top bloke, a very nice man and very caring; he took me out in his car, then he used to stand at the bus stop with me at about 8 pm and put me on the bus that went down my street. When I got in, Mum never asked where I'd been. For her, the main thing was that I was out of the house, and as long as I was back in for 9 pm, it was okay.

I had a friend who lived a couple of doors away and we used to get up to a load of mischief. We went to the shop and dropped our money over the other side of the counter so the old man had to bend down to pick it up, and then we could fill your pockets with anything we could reach. That was the only way of getting sweets. We also went to the pub up the road and I climbed over the wall and passed empty bottles over to my mate. He'd put them in a carrier bag and then we'd take them into the pub to get the refund. You got 2 pence on small brown bottles and 5 pence on the large pop bottles, so, on a good day, we could get close to a pound. We then went to the shop and asked for some sweets off the back shelf and while the man's back was turned, we stole some of the chocolate on the counter. Also, because I was short and thin, I could get my hand down the side of the glass cabinet and get bars of chocolate.

We'd spend most of our evenings walking round the posh houses at the top of the road. It was a huge estate with some very big houses that were worth millions, and we would climb over the fences and go into the gardens to take clothes off the washing lines. When they had dirty shoes and trainers outside the back door, we would sit down and try them on; if they fitted, we just tied the laces together and put them around our necks, then climbed over into the next garden to see what was there. Some nights you could get some nice T-shirts and jumpers off the washing line, and the odd time you'd get some shorts or tracksuit bottoms, but it was very rare to get jeans. You'd hit the jackpot if you got a coat; even if it was wet and dirty, it was a top find! This went on for a few years and dark nights were best for doing it. The next morning, I'd sit in my back garden with a bucket of soapy water washing the trainers and shoes and anything else that was good. I'd give them all a wash and hang them out to dry. We often went to jumble sales – about 12 to 16 of us – and steal everything we got our hands on, even down to hats and walking sticks. Since we were small, the bigger lads would push us under the table then make a fuss so the lady would concentrate on them and not us; you got some good coats from there. A lot of the time they'd chase us out because we could get under the tables and get to the cash tins at the back, then grab what we could out of the tins.

In the summer, we'd all go out on the bikes we'd built ourselves using old bikes from the rubbish tip. We would take home all the parts, strip off what we wanted and then take the other bits back on the next visit. We would ride for miles on a nice hot day, with just a pair of shorts on. No one had brakes on their bike; you used your left foot to push against the rear tyre, which fucked up your trainers, but that was the only way to stop. Some nights, we'd go to the youth club – it was great in there – but we were allowed in only from 4 pm till 6 pm, then the 12-year-olds went in. I always tried to sneak back in and play a bit longer, but when they saw you, you had to leave or get banned. Also, in summer, we used to go into the fields when they were cutting the wheat and baling hay; they let us go in the hay dragger and pulled us around, then we'd climb on the trailer when they were stacking the bales of hay and hang off the back all the way to the farm. It was just like what we use to do in the evenings when we'd wait for the bus to stop and open the flaps on the back of the bus, then hang on for around 2 miles or get off when it stopped, but then we either had to wait for 30 minutes for the next bus or walk home.

By the time I'd hit the age of eight, my life was still the same at home, but in the school summer holidays, I started my own window cleaning round. I had 36 houses to do at 15 pence per house, so I earned the huge sum of £5.40 a week. All I had was a tall wooden ladder that was heavy. Some customers were great and offered you a glass of juice; others were just miserable old gits. When you'd done the upstairs window, they would go into the bedroom to check and point to the corners and then ask you to clean the window sills as well; they wanted blood for 15 pence. Some days it was roasting hot but they didn't give a toss about you. They'd tell you to do the small window on the upstairs landing, but this was almost impossible to reach. They didn't give a fuck though; they wanted that window cleaned or you didn't get paid, but some of them said, "Don't do that one, luv, it's too dangerous." I'd get my round done anyway and I'd get sunburned, as all I had on was a pair of shorts. Then I'd put the ladder away and my Mum would take the £5 and leave me with the 40 pence, but that was a lot of money for me to play with back then.

We never went on family holidays like everyone else at school did; we couldn't afford it as ours was such a big family. That meant we all had to make our own fun like going on a long bike ride or swimming over at the sailing club or in the reservoir. We had to be out of the house all day anyway, otherwise Mum would boot us out. It was hard enough trying to go in for a drink of water – she wouldn't let you in even for that. If we were going swimming over at the canal, we'd look in the bin for an empty bottle and one of the lads would take it home to wash it and fill it with water.

When I was little, I had to walk home from school; it was a long way so I would try to tag onto someone who lived near me and see if the Mum would get me any sweets when she got them for her own kids. They didn't, but it was safer to walk home behind one of the Mums. When I got home, Mum said:

"Get that school uniform off and put your old stuff on!"

I'd just put my pants, T-shirt and top over the door on the water-heater cupboard in the bathroom, and put on the stuff I'd been wearing all week. Then I was sent out. We didn't have many clothes and not one bedroom had a wardrobe, so I have no idea what the girls use to do with their clothes, but the point was that the boys had to get changed and leave the house after school, while the girls peeled spuds and helped do the tea, which was always the same. If you were in the kitchen, you could make a chip butty and eat it and then get another slice of bread and go back into the front room to finish your tea and that was it. You knew your next meal would be tea the next night, as we weren't given any breakfast. I used to take raw sausages out of the fridge to put in my pocket and then eat them cold outside. At the weekend, Mum would go to get her hair done and bring some pies home, but you weren't allowed to eat any, and she would bring two cakes and tell you not to touch them as they were for our dad, so you had no chance. It wasn't only me that didn't get enough to eat though; a few of my mates used to nip in and grab a sugar butty, which is something I've never tried. Some of them got dinner but you could tell the ones who didn't as they were left outside playing and waiting for the lucky ones to come back. Sometimes, one would bring food out and we were like vermin surrounding him and asking for a bite. Some would give you a bite, but then everyone wanted one until the food had all gone.

Anyway, one day, I went to school and it was sunny and hot, and one of the lads who I didn't play with, but who I use to talk to in class, asked me to wag school with him (to play truant) and I agreed. It was a very early age to play truant but the school never checked back then, so we walked to the big park a couple of miles away. It was a Friday and he said he could get us some money because people wanted extra milk for the weekend and as we walked along, we found empty milk bottles with notes in them on doorsteps. One note said, 'Milkman, please leave one extra pint, the money is under the mat', so we lifted up the mat and bang on; the money got us some food. We ended up across the big park that had a golf course, a huge playground and an animal section. We played for a bit and went to the café, then PN (his initials) said he knew a place where all the sweets and chocolate were stored, so I said,

"Let's go!"

We walked from the park towards St Helen's Hospital and got to the front of the building which had big double doors where vans were filling up and driving off. We tried to get something from the front but got chased off. PN said they closed for dinner and everyone went home, and that he'd broken in before, so I thought, ok, let's go for it, and so we waited till 12 noon. They closed up and we went round and knocked on the door. There was no answer so we went round the back and there were some small windows about 3 metres up. We looked around and got an old wooden ladder off the roof of a garage, climbed up and broke the glass up with a brick. He passed down a box of Mars bars and a box of Flakes, then as we went round the side, we saw police everywhere. We ran through the bushes and through a pond that was half dried up with the sun, but we were struggling to run in the mud so we ditched a lot of the stuff that we could hardly carry. We came out at the other side on the park's 'pitch and put', covered in mud up to our knees and just stood next to three blokes who were playing the game, and walked around with them to each hole. The police arrived and saw us but didn't say anything as we seemed to be with these older men. I have no idea why they didn't pull us because we had mud up to our knees. Anyway, we stayed with the older men until they'd finished, then we walked off to a stream to wash our legs, socks and shoes, and made our way back to school, and I later went home chocolate-free, as I'd either eaten or given away all that I could carry. Mum went mad when I got home. She gave me a good slap across the face a few times and she just went crazy. "What the fuck have you been doing?" she asked. I told her I was getting the ball out of the stream and fell in. She made me go outside and wash my school shoes and socks in a bucket. No one at home normally ever asked how your day had been. I just got changed and went out with the rest of my friends from the estate.

A jumble sale was held in the church hall, run by all the posh people from the estate; we called them The Poshes, and about 12 of us went along. You had to pay to get in and there were loads of people there. We said our Mum was paying, then ran riot around the place, robbing anything and everything. We got jeans, T-shirts, trainers and shoes, and some good coats. I took one of those lumberjack jackets off a rack and stood there with it on looking at the others.

"Can I help, love?" asked the woman.

"I'm just waiting for my Mum," I said.

She walked off and I left with the coat. At that point, all the lads had gathered around one stall with older people's stuff on it and they were all trying things on but the woman was getting pissed off. We needed to distract her so DM could go under the tables and get to the back to take the pound note in her tin. After he'd done that, we put the stuff back and walked off.

As I got through the years at school, I liked it less and less but I still had to go. I was more interested in my window cleaning round just to earn some money, and I even started to work on the milk float, getting up at 5 am and walking around 2 miles to meet Roy, the milkman. He was a big, fat, lazy bastard and he had two of us working for him.

He didn't get up off his fat arse but just shouted,

"32, one silver top; 36, one gold top, one silver top."

I would do one side of the street and Col would do the other. Our street was one of the last streets, so we used to hide bottles of milk in other people's gardens, then pick them up to take home later. You had to hide it so Roy didn't see you though or he'd take it out of your wage on a Friday. Any cash paid for milk or bread fat Roy would pocket. Then, in the summer holidays, we would work with the bread man. He had a huge round and he use to sell all sorts – from bread to bleach to soap – he was a great bloke! I think his name was Brian, and he paid 50p a day. You could also rob sweets from the back of the van, although he had only Polos and other mints for some old girl in the Posh Estate up the road from us.

As I mentioned before, on a night we use to go *lining* around the Posh Estate; winter time was best as it would get dark early. You could still do it in summer but it had to be late. We'd climb over from garden to garden and try on any clothes on the washing line. If they fitted you, that was great and you kept them; if not, you hung them back up. Most of the time, you'd find dirty trainers or shoes outside the back door and so you'd sit down, take yours off and try these on. If they fitted, you tied the laces together and hung them round your neck, then moved on to the next garden. On good nights, we'd put the stash in a safe place and carry on, then collect it on the way home. When you got home, you'd have to hide the clothes until you could tell your Mum your mate had given you something that didn't fit him and the next day, you'd get a bucket of soapy water and scrub the trainers clean – even better if you'd got two pairs – then you'd rinse them and hang them on the line to dry, and again, you told Mum your mate had given you these too.

If it was a good night, you could end up with a coat or one of your mates would give you one that didn't fit them, as we all looked after each other. Everything we got was wet off the line, and the trainers were full of dirt, but we didn't care. It was free stuff and we needed it a lot more than they did.

About six of us were out walking through the Posh Estate one winter night, but it wasn't cold. We'd always start in a different garden and then move on. We'd been out for a couple of hours and there wasn't much about, then we found ourselves in a big back garden with vegetable patches and a load of rhubarb. We'd just taken a couple of things off the line when the kitchen light came on; now, if this happened, the rule was to hit the ground and lie flat, but one lad didn't. The woman shouted and her husband started to unlock the door. A couple of lads got out over the back but there wasn't enough room for us to lie down, so a couple more jumped into the next garden and I lay in the middle of the rhubarb patch in panic mode. The man ran to the back gate and opened it, shouting abuse at the ones running off, then his wife came out and they were both 2 metres away from me, and he was going mad calling us all the names and saying he would call the police.

"Calm down," she told him. "They haven't taken anything; they're just kids playing." Meanwhile, I was lying in the rhubarb with her son's coat on. "Come inside and I'll make you a drink," she said, but he was still shouting, "I'll fucking kill them!"

No one took up her invitation though and I stayed put for about 15 minutes until the kitchen light went off. I counted another 300 in my head, then crawled to the fence and jumped over to the next garden, climbed over their back wall and ran home. My mates were playing in the street and they asked if he'd caught me, so I told them no, I'd just lain quiet. They said they'd looked for me, then thought the man must have caught me. I told them about what had happened in the garden and they laughed. I told them he was fuming; good job he didn't get anyone.

I always tried to earn money by doing anything I could, from going to the shop for people to washing their car. Although there weren't many cars in our street as the council didn't hand them out, I did a few of the ones that were there, and the blokes were great. Then I was asked by another bloke to do this brand-new car; can't remember the make but the car was cream with a chrome grill and bumpers, and chrome mirrors and handles, so I said okay. He asked me how much and we agreed on 50p. He got me water to wet it down, then a bucket of soapy water to clean it, and when I'd finished, water to rinse it and a cloth to dry the car off. It was very hot outside so it was hard work and it took me about 45 minutes as it kept drying very quickly, and I had to keep wetting the car again. After I'd finished, I went and knocked at the house and he walked over, looked round the car and saw there wasn't a mark on it.

"What about the chrome?" he said.

"I've washed and dried it all," I said.

"I need it polished!"

"I don't have anything to use," I said.

"I have," he said.

He came out with a tin of Brasso, so I polished the chrome on the front and back bumpers, on the two mirrors, the front grill and on the four wheel hubs, then let it dry and polished it off with a clean dry cloth. By this time, I'd spent 90 minutes on it. He came back and looked at every little bit of chrome.

"Where's the cloth?" he said, "the badge isn't clean; it has white Brasso on it."
"I gave it back to you."
"Wipe it off with your T-shirt," he said.

I did and then he smirked, gave me 50p and walked off. I was fucking fuming and didn't know whether to put the car windows out or his house windows. After my tea, I was over at the field, playing about with the lads and girls, and I told one of the lads what had happened.

"You should have hit him!" he said.
"Good idea", I replied. "He's 6 foot 4" and I'm just on 4 feet."
"What are you thinking of doing?" he asked.
"I can't pour dirty water all over the car; he'd know it was me."

Anyway, we went into the empty house across the road, and I had a shit in a newspaper, then went to his car, ripped the paper and picked off bits of shit, then shoved it behind the door handles, every one of them. My mate then asked me if I could get under the car and I said it was easy, so I slid under and wiped the rest of the shit onto the back of the radiator. The funny thing was that when I asked him to do one side, he said that he liked me, but not that much. If it was his shit, he said, it would be ok. Thinking about what he'd said, I just kept laughing while I was still under the car. Then he told me to shut up and stay where I was because someone had just come out of his house. He ran back to the empty house and I tried to slide further under the car, but something was blocking me, so I just pulled my legs in and the bloke walked to the car. I thought, 'I'm going to die.' The next thing, his younger brother shouted after him, "Mike, they're here on the sofa!" so he walked back over to the house and went inside. I slid out and ran like fuck. My mate said if he'd started the car, he'd have gone right over me and I told him I couldn't flatten down enough to get to the back. We went back to our mates and just carried on as normal. Some nights, we would lie in the road with our bike across our bodies and with tomato sauce on our face and it worked! Every time a car came, the driver would slam on the brakes and jump out of the car, so you had to get up and race off on your bike before they got to you. Fuck, we had loads of close calls! Then there was the other trick with three on each side of the road pretending to be pulling on a rope across the road. That never failed, and I have no idea how no one ever got killed as a few of the cars mounted the pavement.

In summer, we'd spend most of our time over on the field and across the railway, where there were two huge mental hospitals with a maze of tunnels underneath that went all over the place. All we had was a candle, as no one could afford a torch, so we just managed with that. If you took the right route, you could get to one of the two towers and climb the concrete stairs to the top and come out on the tower roof; it was amazing – around 200 metres high – and you could see for miles. As you came down onto each landing, there was a very big oak door that was locked and when you looked through the keyhole, you could see into the wards and watch the patients, some of them strapped to the bed and screaming. It wasn't nice to see, but as kids, we didn't really understand what was going on. Sometimes you saw how these people were like zombies, just standing staring at the wall. It was creepy. A lot of the patients were let out to walk round the grounds and streets, and the ones that were high on medication just looked blank. A few times when we were walking through the woods to go over, we'd see the men sitting on the ground looking at dirty magazines and masturbating. Still, we did have some great times around there. I remember coming up from a tunnel that came out at the side of the hospital's rear entrance and as we were getting out, some bloke came out shouting, and all the lads ran off. But I was the last one out and didn't see him. I just thought he was a patient and ran past him, but he chased me along the grass. I should have carried on running but I stopped and dodged and turned round, and he slipped and fell; then I saw there was another man at the back of him. My plan was to shoot off into the woods, but the other man grabbed me and I was taken over the road to the next hospital and into the main security office. I thought they were going to call the police.

"Now, young Tucker, what you are doing here?" asked one of the guards, and laughed.

"We were just in the woods and playing on the field, and then we were walking around the hospital when that bloke came out and shouted so I ran. No one here has ever chased us before," I said.

"Don't worry about him and his friend. They're doctors and they're probably having a bad day," he said. "Come with me!"

He took me to the main hospital entrance and told me to go home.

"Thank you, Brian," I said.

"Don't worry, just remember to run faster the next time," he said and laughed again.

Looking back, I remember we spent a lot of time in those tunnels. Someone had said there was a tunnel running from the hospital, under the big field across the road from our house and up to the church at the top of the hill, which the monks had used to get to the church and back, so we spent half our time trying to find this tunnel but we never found it. We looked for it for years. We did find other tunnels though; one came up near the cricket pitch so we started to use that when we were coming out; it took us 120 metres away from the hospital.

I used to knock about with one of the lads in our street who had a 16-year-old brother, and one time, when I knocked for this mate, his brother opened the door and told me to go in, saying that my mate wouldn't be a minute. I went in and sat down then he showed me some mags with nude women in them and I'd not seen anything like that before. He talked about sex and asked me what I knew about it, and I said I knew nothing. He said he'd show me what to do so he took my pants down, laid me on the couch and got on my back. He was a big lad, about 14 stone, and he was hurting me, then someone put a key in the door and he told me to get dressed. He said if I told anyone, the police would take me away.

The next time I was with the brother, I was in the house with my mate, and the older brother sent him to the shop and told me to wait. As I sat there, he told me to take my shorts off and said he'd show me what to do to a woman. I had no idea what was going on, but he was hurting me again, and this time, he had pulled my legs apart and I shouted because it hurt, so he stopped. He tried again and I started to cry. He then told me how the police would take me away from my family for doing that because I was too young, so only me and him could know. I said okay, then, when his brother came back, he asked why I'd been crying and big brother said we'd been playing and he'd caught me in the face with the cushion but that I was fine now. I had to agree with him. After that, we went out and I didn't want to go to his house again so I kept away for weeks. I even played in my own garden until his older brother had walked past, as I was scared to death of him and didn't want the police to take me away. Then I would go and play with my mates, so I didn't see him for a good few months. Then one day, he saw me in the street and asked me to go into the house with him for some lemonade, and, like an idiot, I went. As soon as I got in, he had his pants open and made me do things to him and play with his penis, while he had me standing in front of him with no pants on. After that, I didn't go out for a while because I knew it was my own fault for going there in the first place. A couple of days later, it was the summer holidays, and I was playing in the street, and I saw The Beast walking down the street towards me. I shit myself because I couldn't get to my house and the only thing I could do was crawl under one of the cars, so I lay under the car and saw that he'd stopped to talk to one of his friends. I was under there for a long time, and it started to get cold but I didn't want to come out. They finally finished talking and he walked home but I waited until he had walked through his gate, then I crawled out and went home and didn't go out for a couple of days; I just played at the side of my house. My friends were asking me to come out but I was too scared to leave because I didn't want to go through this again. I even thought of killing him just so I could start to play out again.

Then I changed friends and started to go around with lads from the other streets. I wanted to keep away from the lads in our street because I knew this was going to happen again, but a lot of the time, I just stayed in my own garden playing with a tennis ball I'd found at school and had taken home with me. I used to throw it on the roof and catch it until it got stuck in the gutter then I had to climb up and get it back. It was strange how one person could change your life and put a stop to everything you used to do as a child.

Then one day, my older brother made a golf club out of some copper pipe; it was about 2 inches thick. He took his time to bend it, then sat it on a big stone and hammered the face flat to hit the ball. We all had other bits of bent pipe but nothing like his! We would go over to the field and he'd let you have a go of it; it was awesome that you could hit the ball a good distance and just with a handmade club! That took up a lot of our time through the day. Then, when I was around 10, I found a couple of golf clubs in the gardens on the Posh Estate, so we decided to go and get some golf balls from the private course near us. Wow – this place was full of posh money wankers who would spot us, but we found loads of golf balls in the farmers' fields nearby. We didn't mind getting undressed to go into a ditch and root through the mud. It smelled like shit, but we got loads of balls and went into the stream to get washed and clean the balls. You still had the smell of the ditch but, if you picked some dock leaves and flowers, you could wash yourself down with them and get rid of most of the smell. I learned this from my older brother as they used to do it in the morning when they had camped out. They also got a small branch half-an-inch thick, peeled off the bark and chewed the end, then rubbed the stick with some stinging nettles or chewed the nettles, and used the stick to clean their teeth.

There was an area near us which we called the 'big field'. There were two rugby pitches and about four football pitches with plenty more land around the field. One of the lads went right round the outside on his motorbike and it measured a mile. He did this for my lovely neighbour who had greyhounds and used to walk them 5 times around the field. He did this at 5 am before work, and at 6 pm after his tea. He was a great bloke and a big personality too; he was really missed when he passed away.

So, on the big field, we then made our own golf course and got a petrol lawnmower from someone's dad to cut the green. The grass was cut every week by the council so it was already fairly short. We had only 3 holes but they were good to play. To make the hole, we got an empty beans tin and stamped it into the ground then got it out with a screwdriver. It left a perfect hole. We even got flags from the posh course and put one in each hole to make it look good. Roy, the posh lad who played with us, was 6 feet 3 inches tall, but fuck me, he was 14 and still a baby. He was four years older than me then. One Saturday, I went to the town with him to look at golf clubs in a shop that sold them cheap, second-hand, and also sold golf balls, so I picked up a ball for each of us, and put one in my pocket and one in his. After we'd left the shop, and got about 50 metres away, the bloke grabbed us, dragged us back to the shop and took the balls back. He then put us in his car and took us home, with Roy crying all the fucking way home, and went in to see Roy's dad, then went in with me, as I lived 4 doors away, but as luck would have it, my dad was at work so it was my Mum. She agreed with him, said sorry, and told him I'd be kept in, then smacked me around the face a couple of times. The guy was happy and off he went, and Mum said,

"Now, get the fuck out of my sight and go outside; don't come back till 5 pm."

That was our normal time for tea. As I've said, we didn't get any breakfast or dinner; only 'tea' as we use to call it, and we'd try to hide some bread under our plates. If you went in at any other time, she would shout:

"What you doing in?"

"Just getting a drink of water," you would say, grabbing a couple of rounds of bread to take with you.

Meanwhile, I struggled with the flashbacks of what my mate's brother did to me, and I always thought when I got older, I'd go and confront him about it and stab him. I was still a little young, but this feeling didn't go away.

Then I was back for my last years at junior school. I used to walk home before then, but now I walked the 2½ miles going to school as well. I got 5 pence for the bus and that got me chips at dinner time and left me a penny, so loads of us would go into the sweet shop, and it was crazy how we would confuse the old lady, and when I say old, I mean she was around 75 or 80 years old. We'd pinch what we could and it was funny to watch. We would ask,

"Can I have a quarter of those sweets on the shelf?"

We wanted the sweets at the back of the second shelf, which was quite high up, so she got her little steps out and as she went up, there were fucking hands everywhere; we were like a pack of hyenas, then she would weigh them out and say:

"That's 2 pence."

"Oh God, I've lost my other money; sorry, I only have a penny," you'd say.

When she went to put the sweets back in the jar, then went up again to put the jar back, it was like a dog fight as we tried to get sweets from the counter. She didn't have a clue about what was missing. Then we would all go outside and share what we had, and even the lads who wouldn't go into the shop because they were scared still got some.

We used to go to the Big Show in Sherley Park and spent most of the time lifting up the canvas at the back of the tents to see what we could grab. We'd go to this huge beer tent and do the same; just lift up the sheet and if someone was sitting on the grass with their pint beside them, we'd take it and share it. We could spend hours behind the beer tent because it got easier as time went on, so we all ended up drunk.

When I was younger, I was a proper pretty boy and all the girls wanted to go out with me, but it didn't interest me; then we got a new neighbour who had a few kids. I think I was about 16 and the oldest girl was 5 or 6 years older than me, but wow, she was absolutely stunning! She was nice and slim, and very pretty. Anyway, one day I was walking round to the field and she stopped me at the end of the street.

"Where you are going, love?" she said.

"Over to the big field," I said.

"Come for a walk with me," she said.

I said okay and we walked up the road. She asked if I had a girlfriend and I said no.

"Would you like to kiss me?" she asked.

Fuck me, it was like all my Christmases had come at once and she showed me how to do French kisses. Wow, what a day! That was when the masturbating started. A few times she got me and kissed me for a good long time; I wish I'd known about sex because she was all over me. I couldn't tell anyone as no one would believe me. She was 17 years old and hot and I was about 11. I used to stand at the side of their house and wait for her to come out and we'd walk along the field. She would sit on the ground and teach me how to kiss; it was amazing. She pulled me on top of her a couple of times and she would say she could feel how excited I was getting, but I had no idea what the next move was, so I just enjoyed this many times and it happened because she was absolutely stunning. I used to wish I was older, but never mind. Everyone was talking about her and they used to ask me what I thought, and I'd say I thought she was stunning. I knew if I'd said anything more, they'd have laughed at me so I kept it secret and waited for it to happen again. By this time, I was seeing a very pretty girl from the top of the hill, but I was still in love with my pretty neighbour. There was no way it would go anywhere, I knew, but I still had hope.

The neighbour ended up with a fellow who was thin and ugly, so that was me done. I went back to my mates, picking carrots in the farmers' fields and sitting beside the stream eating and talking shit. Most of the time we'd go into the farmers' fields and grab some carrots, wash them in the stream and then all sit round eating them. On a night, we'd go to a different field and dig up some potatoes, make a fire and put the spuds on the fire, then bite off the black from the outside and eat the white part inside. Most of my mates did the same, and we'd also set snares to catch rabbits the odd time. If we got one, we'd skin it with a stick; all you had to do was rip its stomach, peel the skin back, pull out the guts then push your fingers round the body under the skin and pull the body out just like pulling a jumper that's inside out, then cut off the feet, head and tail and put the stick through its bum and through its mouth; then it was ready to hang over the fire. We'd get more spuds and carrots, wrap the carrots in dock leaves and put it all on the fire. The leaves stopped you from setting fire to the carrots. After that, we all tucked in and it was lovely! As people say, life is what you make it. I had loads of friends and we all used to all look after each other and help each other even when we were all shoplifting or looking for clothes on washing lines in the back gardens of the posh houses. No one was left out and that's loyalty.

I went back to playing rugby when I was about 10 years old and played for a local team. Billy had got it all going and he'd done a good job; nice bloke as well. We had a night match just over the field against Hare and Hounds. We were only a small team, but fuck me, some of them had facial hair so Billy asked their age and they said they were 14, but what the fuck. They beat us, but one big thing was my family were all huge rugby players and all my brothers played, so my dad came over to watch the match. I had no idea he was there; it was a summer night, and he was watching the game then going for a pint with his mate. Anyway, I was playing number 9, so I was in the middle of the field and just on the halfway line, they passed the ball left all the way to the wing man, who was in an open space; he'd gone 5 metres before I set off, so I sprinted back and dived for him, hitting him halfway up his body and he dropped the ball and ended up in touch. The crowd went crazy shouting for me. After the game, when we were all walking off, my dad came over to me and patted me on the head.

"Well done, lad, that was outstanding!" he said.

That is something I'll never forget in my life. Even now, at the age I am, thinking back to that moment still makes me feel so proud that I'd pleased my dad in that game. He wasn't like other Dads; he didn't show emotions or ever give us a hug or a kiss; he never told us he loved us, but he was a great man who worked very hard all his life. He was also very well-respected throughout the town and everyone knew him. They even called me 'Young Tuck' after his nickname and that was the name most people knew me by. I had loads of good mates; we did everything together, went everywhere together and always looked out for each other no matter what. If we took something, we would share it, if we got something and sold it, we'd split the money and no one was ever left out. We were always having a laugh and we played some type of game most nights and had two teams, and it could get a bit rough, but they were your mates. They always picked you up if you had been flattened or if they cut you or anything, someone always had a rag or something in their pocket to put over the wound until you went to hospital to get it stitched. We had a pylon in the big field, and it was big, but we used to get through the barbed wire and climb onto the pegs then race to the top. It was around 180 to 200 feet high, and it was only when you were up there that you thought, 'shit, I have to climb back down' and it was harder getting down than going up. We spent hours playing on it and we even had a huge swing in the middle. It was the same at home when you got onto the roof; you climbed up the drainpipe onto the gutter and over to the roof and then you could walk across the block of 4 houses, but the hardest part was getting back down because you had to grip the gutter from the roof then spin yourself round and hang onto the gutter until your feet found the drainpipe. Mum used to shout at us for doing that but if Dad had known, he would have given us the belt as he didn't like you doing anything dangerous or anything where you could get hurt.

Before I was 11 years old, I had a thing about electrics and when I was alone at home, I opened the meter cupboard and looked at the meter. I thought if you put 10p in there, it must drop into the box at the bottom. There was a round brown bolt on each side but it had wire going through it and was sealed with lead, which kept the two sides together, so I got a knife from the kitchen and started to push it into the lead seal. I managed to open it and so the wire came off one side; then I did the other side. It took me over an hour to do that. I took the seals off and unscrewed the brown flat nuts with holes in the outside and when I took them both off, the front part of the meter came away and there was a slot in the top of the box a lot bigger than a piggy bank slot. I put the knife inside it and turned the meter upside down, then 10 pence pieces started to fall out, so I took about 10 of them out, then wondered what would happen if I put it in without the front part, so I tried one and it just fell through but the meter registered the coin, so I put it through a few times to build up the time to cover the missing money. Then I put it all back and put the screws on then the seals, and fitted the wire back into each seal. I did that once every few months until they changed to 50p and fitted new seals, but I got those off too. A while after that, Mum asked me to go to my sister and ask her to lend her some money.

"I can get you some money," I said, "but you mustn't go mad at me."

"How can you do that?" she asked.

"You're not damaging that!" she said when I took her to the meter.

"No, I saw my friend do it," I said.

I took the front of the meter off while she was there, and it was full; the electricity was a rip-off.

"How much do you want?"

"Just get £5 out."

I got it out and told her the meter was still full, so I got her another £5 out, then she told me to get 50p for myself. I got one and put it into the meter, turned it, and the coin fell back out.

"How many times can you do that?" she asked me.

"Why?"

"If you can do it a couple of times, I wouldn't have to put any money in for a couple of days!"

I put the coins back in until the dial went to the top, and then I put the meter back together.

"Don't let this go any further," she said. "Don't tell your brother or sister or your friend. It's just between me and you," she said.

I said okay and then went outside. That day, she was like a real mum; she made me a sandwich and got me a drink, but the day after, everything was back to normal; she wasn't nice and was always making threats and hitting me. Then, the month after, she wanted money out of the meter again. It wasn't till I was older that I realised I was getting her free electricity, but nothing was ever said when the meter man came to empty the box. He just counted the money, put it in bags and off he went; so, I did this for a few years until they changed the meter and that was the end of it, as this one had double seals and you couldn't open it up to free the wire.

I had finally made it to high school and had a uniform that was too big. Also, I was the only one out of 1100 pupils wearing a blue blazer as everyone else had a black one, but no, fucking dark blue was cheaper so she got me that; she should have got a white one because I stood out like a prick.

FROM 12 TO 14 YEARS OLD WITH THE BLUE BLAZER

After I started at the big school, I still had some friends from my old school who I got along with, but a lot of people kept away from me because I was from the council estate. When we had games or sports, I wore the boots I stole from my old school, and I didn't have a school sports bag; I used a plastic carrier bag and wore the same pair of shorts I'd been wearing for years. After a while, I started to stay behind for a bit in the changing room and was the last one out, so if anyone left anything, I would pick it up; a tie, a jumper, socks or anything; even soap because Mum didn't give us soap for school. I did think of taking someone's sports bag but they would know so I had to keep trying at the jumble sales. I was working every weekend for my brother's company and he was not a nice person to work for. You got picked up at 7.45 am and dropped off at 4.30 pm on Saturday and Sunday and he would pay me £xx, £10 of which I had to give to my mum, but the odd time, when I had to go to the shop for all the lads, I would make a couple of pounds out of the change. This I kept under my bottom drawer; I was saving up for a sports bag, but when my older brother left school and gave me his bag, I was made up! I spent all night cleaning it, ready for school. The only problem then was that Mum wouldn't let me take a towel, so I had to put an extra T-shirt in the bag to dry myself. However, after a few months I ended up finding a towel and I took it home, washed it and used that for sports. Then, when I got home, I'd put it on the washing line to dry. A few of the bigger lads would call me about the football boots but I just said I liked them; that was until we were out looking around the Posh Estate for washing left out and one night, I found a pair of Puma football boots. They were covered in mud but I tried them on and they fitted me. That was great! There was also a pair of trainers caked in mud at the side so I just took them as well. It was a good night. I got a couple of T-shirts and a jumper, and I got my football boots and a new towel. It was like winning the jackpot! Next day, I sat in my back garden and took all the mud off the boots and trainers, and gave them a wash. They were beautiful and they had metal studs too. I loved the sound of the studs when I got changed and I felt like part of the group.

My old boots had rubber studs and I wanted metal ones but you couldn't change them, so I knocked small nails into each stud just to make the right sound when I walked. It didn't work out though because all the nails came out of the studs during training and playing rugby. I was gutted but just had to get on with it. My friends would come in wearing boots and they looked amazing. It was something I would dream about but could never afford, and, if I did buy a pair, Mum would make me take them back and get the money back.

My brother told me I didn't need to worry about the extra hours I was working, but that I should worry about moving all the rubble instead. It wasn't like any other Saturday job. I worked with him for a long time and it was very hard work. He treated me like dirt; he would come out with a cup of tea or coffee and not bother getting anything for me. He was very selfish. Then he got hold of me one Saturday and said, "I want you to climb up on this roof, go in through the roof window and open the door." When I asked why, he said, "Just get the fucking door open!" I climbed onto the roof around 40 feet up and got through the window, then climbed down the racking inside. The place was full of small appliances. When I opened the door, he came in and took loads of boxes, and told me to keep putting them in the van until it was full. Then he closed the door and patted me on the head, and said, "Well done, kid!"

After this, he dropped me off at home around 6.30 pm.

"See you tomorrow", he said and drove off.

The day after, we were back finishing the concrete and having to mix it ourselves because it was Sunday. It was a killer. I was covered in cement and it was starting to get dark when he shouted me over and told me to get on the roof again and open the door for him after the lads had left. I did what he said and then he loaded the van again like before, but this time, he just dropped me off at the corner of the street and said he'd see me the next week.

"What about my money?"

I thought he was going to give me extra but he gave me two five-pound notes.

"Don't I get anything for all the boxes?" I asked.

He got out a huge wad of notes and gave me two one-pound notes.

"Wow!" I said. "Giving me two pounds more has nearly killed you!"

He snatched them back and gave me a slap.

"You're lucky you have a job," he said. "Now fuck off!"

Then I just went home, gave Mum the money and had a cold shower in the garden using the hosepipe because she wouldn't put the hot water on for you. I knew there was no one I could tell about what had happened. I would just have to put up with getting extra money from the lads for going to the shop for them, so I went to meet them all to plan our next money-making scheme.

Most of my mates from junior school came to our school; it wasn't far from my house and we started on the Tuck Shop in the break. Two pupils ran the shop, and we would climb through the window at the back and rob the sweets out of the boxes behind the two girls. Yes, we finally got caught and – wow – six swipes on the hand with a cane fucking hurts! You would struggle to write after you were finished, and everyone in the class would want to look at your hand to see the bruises. There were 5 of us in the class who stuck together and most weeks, two or three or all of us got caned. I remember going with Alan when he'd put 4 books down the back of his pants and I thought 'you'll never get away with that; it sticks out a mile!' Yes, we were caught and were sent to the headmaster. He asked if we wanted 3 on the hand or 6 on the arse. I went first and bent over – fuck, he must have taken a run-up because it really hurt, and I had to stand there while Alan was getting done. Then we had to apologise and go back to the class, but we used to go the toilets first to show each other our arses and see how many bruise lines we had. I dropped my pants and Alan seemed surprised.

"Fuck me, Tuck, that looks shocking; you have blue lines running across your arse!" he said.

We started laughing and then he took his down and I was gutted – not a mark! I still had to admire him for doing it though.

"It was great," he said, "I didn't feel a thing!"

Looking back, I remember that even when I was young, we always had a code: 1) Never steal from your own kind; 2) Never take anyone's tools and 3) Never break into anyone's house. I obeyed these rules throughout my life, and I can honestly say I have never broken the code. Yes, we took what we could but that was from big companies and from the back of very big houses, and we only ever broke into shops or warehouses, so this code stayed with me all my life and everyone I use to knock about with stuck to it too. I remember the house of one of the old people in the street had been broken into and we found out who'd done it, so the older lads got him, took him over to the field, then kicked him all over the place. They even made him get the stuff he'd taken and the money out of the meter and take it back to the old lady. There were around 12 of us standing at the gate when he knocked and apologised, and handed everything back to her. She was crying and when the lad came up the steps, John smacked him on the jaw and he fell over, then me and Win walked down to her to see if she was okay, and she was so upset she rang her son. We waited for him to come and she was so grateful I felt like crying myself. Her son came in and he started to shout but she stopped him and told him about what we'd done. He thanked us and offered us some money, but we said it was okay, and that we just wanted to make sure his mum was alright. We chatted for a bit and when we left, I said,

"Do you mind if I call the odd time to see if you're okay?"

"Tucker," she said, "you can come anytime you like, sweetheart!"

She gave me a hug, and then we went. I stuck to my word and I would knock on her door and get stuff from the shop for her, and the odd time I would go to sit inside for a bit. She would tell me about her husband and we became good friends. The funny thing was that each time we used to go robbing potatoes from the farm, I always called to Mrs Forbes, the old lady's house, with a bag and tell her they were from my mate's allotment but I think she had a feeling they weren't because I also dug up a load of carrots for her from the farm field across the road, but she was great! I always gave her a big hug and I wished that she was my mum because she was lovely. Her daughter lived a long way away from her and didn't go to see her much, so I tried to be as nice as I could, and if she was in her garden, where she had some nice roses, I used to go in and help her cut the grass. She would make some lemonade and cake and we'd sit down, then she'd tell me more about her husband and we had a couple of laughs as well. I hated it when I had to leave, but I always made sure she was safe. Every time I passed her house, I would stop and get a shopping list, then go to the shop. She always offered me some money but I never took it and she used to go mad if I went back and told her I hadn't paid for something, like the large block of cheese I once got. She would say I'd get myself into trouble, and that she wasn't worth all those favours, but she was. Her home was very nice and the garden was done nicely; she did everything her husband had done and she was trying to keep the garden the same, but I knew she was struggling and that's why I used to help. Once, when we were sitting in her front room, she said,

"I wish I had a son like you!"

"You don't need one; you've got me," I told her. "Don't worry, I'm going nowhere."

She smiled and I could see a tear in her eye behind her glasses, so I changed the subject.

"Right, what do we need to do next?" I asked.

"It's all done, love," she said.

I went outside and took her washing off the line and helped her fold everything and she said,

"Don't let your mum know you're doing this."

"I know," I said, "but you're my Mum!"

She gave me a huge smile. I visited Mrs F. a lot as I didn't want her to be alone too much, but one day when I knocked on the door, her daughter answered. I asked if her mum was in and she told me she was out.

"What do you want?"

"I normally go to the shops for her," I said.

"She doesn't need anything," she answered.

She gave me a horrible look and closed the door, so I didn't call for a couple of days. When I did see Mrs F., she said her daughter was very bossy and wanted her to move house because she was on her own here.

"I told her I was fine and that you'd been helping me, but she didn't seem pleased."

The next thing I knew, my favourite old lady, Mrs F., went into an old folk's home and I really did miss her. I often wondered what it would have been like if I could have left my home and moved in with Mrs F. instead. It would have been a nicer place to live and away from all the shouting. I did try to find out where she had moved to but no one would tell a little lad where an old lady had gone, even though all I wanted to do was visit her and see if she was okay.

Coming home from school, the first thing Mum would say was,

"Take those school clothes off and get changed; then get out, and don't come back until I shout you."

It was strange because all my mates used to go home and their mum would make them a snack before tea, and they had more than one set of school clothes. I think we were stuck in the time of rationing in the 1940s. She would come out and shout for the three of us to go, starting in order with the oldest first, then she'd work her way down. When you went past her at the gate, she would give you a smack on the back of the head for nothing; then you had to sit on the floor to eat your tea of chips and beans, and you might get an egg the odd time, but you weren't allowed any bread and you didn't get a drink. We used to leave a few chips because as soon as we'd finished, we had to go back outside, so we'd take our plates into the kitchen, have a cup of water, then get some bread – it was great if you could get two slices and put your chips on the dry bread, then run outside and eat it. But if you got caught getting the bread, she would take it off you, put it back and drop your chips into the rubbish bag. She was not a nice person. It was like being in prison except that here, you got the same meal every night. It was strange because some of your mates would go home at around 8 pm and tell their mum they were hungry and she'd make them a sandwich. Fuck me, when they brought it out, we were like a pack of wolves all trying to get a bit of this sandwich.

Even at night, she'd be at the gate at 9 pm to shout you in and hit you again as you passed. If we sat down when we went in, she would say,

"What you doing? Piss off and get to bed!"

We'd go into the kitchen and try to get a round of bread, then fold it and shove it down your pants, then go to the sink for a drink. When she came in and asked what you were doing, you had to say you were just getting a drink of water and she would stand and watch you drink it. The funny thing was that if you up picked a cup to put the water in, she'd shout,

"Don't use that cup; I've just washed it!"

So, you had to drink from the tap and then she would shout,

"Come on, hurry up and get upstairs, you little bastard!"

She'd then smack you round the head. If it was the school holidays, you had to be up and out of the house for 9.30 am. You got a drink of tea the odd time but no breakfast, so you'd just go out on the street and wait for your mates to come out, or, if you could, you'd go into their house and try to get a slice of toast from their mum before we went out looking for anything that could earn us some money. That meant we could go to the shop to buy a few sweets, and try to steal some biscuits to keep us going for the day because our meal wasn't until 5 pm, so you had to fill up on that as nothing else would be coming your way.

I was old enough to go to the youth club at the later time now, so this started a new chapter in my life. Most of my mates would go from 7 pm until 10 pm every weeknight, and it was closed at weekends. I made loads of new friends and learned loads of new scams along the way. There was a big snack bar there but you had no chance of getting behind it, and Mrs Bowes, the lady who served, was lovely. She wouldn't allow you to swear near her, but she was a great lady. I only ever had enough money to pay myself in, so I couldn't buy any sweets or get a drink, but the odd time, Mrs Bowes would say,

"Here, love, have this tea!"

Everyone respected her, right from the bottom up to the top nutcases who came in, aged 20, just out of jail, and I even ended up friends with them. There were two big snooker rooms and they started to lock the door from the inside, which led to people messing about and a couple of fights over money, and one of the lads using a snooker cue to hit someone; but you had to defend yourself or die. Sometimes we'd go into the sports hall and play a game called Murder Ball, which was played using a big heavy medicine ball and it *was* heavy. There was a mat at each end where you'd have goals, and the two teams tried to even out the rough-hitters with some all-out crazy bastards in each team. You used any method at all to get the ball onto the opponents' mat to get one point. The game took 4 x 10 minutes with a 5-minute break, which you really needed because it was so brutal a lot of the time, and they often had to phone for an ambulance. It was a tough game, and I know that by the time I was in my teens, the game got harder, and you were playing with people who were 17 and 18 years old. The staff would blow a whistle to separate two people knocking shit out of each other or when the ball was on the mat. I had some great times, especially as I could really smash the odd person I didn't like. There were no fouls in the game, so it just continued until the assistant blew the whistle. Even if people were fighting, he'd let them tire themselves out, or if things were going too far, he'd blow the whistle and stop them, and give them a cloth to clean off the blood, and then the game went on. As I said, it was brutal, but I loved it, and most days, I'd go to school with a black eye.

At that age, I had a thing about keys. I don't know why, but I use to collect them and the odd time I would find one from my bunch of keys that would fit a door we were trying. At the youth club, the door to the storeroom where the sweets were kept was in the snooker room so we booked the snooker room. My mate kept hitting balls while I tried to open the door. It took me a few minutes, but I opened it, and we got a box of Mars bars and a box of Marathons. I opened the window and climbed out, and he passed them to me, then I put them on the roof, climbed back in and locked the door, but then I realised it was best to put the keys on the roof too, so I went out of the window again, and was around 30 feet up, hanging on with one hand. The reason for this was when you came out of the snooker room, you were checked to see if you'd put a ball in your pocket to hit someone with when you got out.

The club was shut over the summer, so we amused ourselves by going over the park, and that's when I tried solvent abuse as we had nothing else to do until it got dark. There would be around 15 to 20 of us under the railway bridge all sniffing glue or lighter fuel. It was crazy to do it every night, but it seemed the normal thing to do. I was lucky in a way because my Mum smoked, and my dad had no sense of smell, so they couldn't pull me on it. I remember going on the glue one Sunday afternoon after I'd bought a big bag of white chocolate buttons and when I got home, I was at the back of the house being sick into the grid and Dad walked round. He gripped me round the throat and lifted me up, and said,

"If I ever find out you've been using any drugs, I'll kill you!"

"No, I haven't," I said. "I've just had some chocolate and I've been playing rugby over on the field and it's made me sick."

Looking back now, I'm ashamed of what I did because my dad was amazing, and I let him down. You'll understand this when you discover that I lost him a few years later.

No one on the estate where I grew up owned a bike of any sort, and if one of my mates came from school on one, we all use to pester him to have a go, so everyone would be riding this lad's bike, but he'd get it back, in the end, to go home. Anyway, one time, when it was summer, me and all the lads on the estate made their own bikes as we couldn't afford to buy one. We used to go down to the tip at Whiston and over to the big tip in St Helens and bring back old bikes, so everyone had one to fix up, and we even gave each other parts; all we needed was a puncture kit and a pump and away we went. One night, when we went up to the Posh Estate and had a walk round, we saw a Grifter bike with a combination lock on it and the lads all looked at me, so I sat at the side of it, and it took me less than a minute to open the lock and we took the bike and took it in turns to use it. Like a dickhead, I took it home and put it in the rear garden. My dad was the most honest man you could ever meet, and when he saw the bike, he shouted over to me,

"Whose is this bike?"

"Paul out of the avenues was with us yesterday playing over at the back field. It's his," I answered quickly. "So, make sure it goes back tomorrow!" he said.

I took it out and told my mates:

"I don't want it anymore because my dad will drag me to the police station!"

We ditched the bike as we couldn't use any of its parts because it was smaller than our bikes, though we did use the wheels on the back of our new Tut-Tut, which, for those who don't know, is a long plank with two wheels at the front and two at the back. You steer it with your feet sort of like a pedal car but this was big enough for grown-ups. We'd got this huge plank; it was inches wide, 4 inches thick and 14 feet long; so, we made one very big, long Tut-Tut. You steered it like the old carts with a foot on either side of the plank which was connected to the wheels. Sounds easy? Please, try it! We went over the road to a nice estate with a steep hill and nine of us got on it and started to go down, going over 25 miles an hour – it was flying! Then, as we came to the first corner, the twins were at the front and it turned the corner and hit the next kerb, then went in the air and turned over. It threw a couple of lads off and landed on top of a few others. One of the twins was stuck because the 6-inch nail used as a turn pin had gone into his leg.

"Fuck, that hurt!" he said as he pulled his leg off the nail.

It was unreal and we all pissed ourselves laughing, then we took the Tut-Tut into the woods and burned it. As we were near the farm field with potatoes, we put spuds on the fire and sat in the woods until around 9 pm, telling stories. Another day, about halfway through the summer holidays, we all decided to go swimming in the lake just past the woods. We often went there when it was warm. We'd pick some carrots, get a loaf of bread and a few bottles of milk from a doorstep, and stay there until around 4 pm, then walk home for tea, and then all meet up around 6 pm and decide what we were going to do for the rest of the night. One night, one of the lads said,

"I went into the big electrical store with our kid today for a radio; you want to see some of the stuff in there, and I was wondering if we could do a mass shop." (That meant everyone in the shop at the same time to confuse the staff, but the shop was so big it would need more than 20 of us and we couldn't get everyone together on the days we wanted. We all went in and had a look round anyway, and I said to DH:

"Look up!"

"At what?"

"Skylights, plastic, cut them or kick them in."

"It's 40 feet high! How do we get up and how do we get down?"

"Going up will be easy, and we can use a rope for going down. I go first and you follow, as we are the smallest. We tie the stuff and lift it to the roof."

"Good idea, mate," said DH. "But who has a rope that long? We used the last one to make the swing on the big tree and the wall."

"We'll have to go to the transport company later tonight," I said.

As we'd been there before for ropes, we knew what to do. You had to stand some lads at one side of the yard behind the fence and climb over the fence on the opposite side of the yard so the dogs stayed near your friends; then, you had to run as fast as you could to get to the back of the trailer before the guard dogs saw you. Once you got another rope from the back of one of the other trailers, you made your way to the other side of the yard where your mates were standing and quickly got back over the fence. The two big guard dogs made it feel like Russian roulette. That night, we decided we'd all walk down to the tip to see if there were any bikes or bike parts, and the transport company was just across the road. We spent over an hour going around the tip as loads of bikes had been dumped. We got what we wanted and put it to one side. Then we went over the road and tried to work out how to get the rope.

It was still daylight and the guard dogs were in the yard, and all the trailers were parked in a line. It wasn't easy as they were in the middle of the yard so it was a good 40 metres to get to a trailer from the fence. Two of the lads went to the front gate and started to make a noise to get the dogs to go to the gate, then I climbed over the fence and waited until they lifted a hand so I could start my run to the trailer. You take your life in your own hands but when you run across the transport yard, and normally you would move along doggy-style so you could see the guard dogs from under the wagon. One of the lads at the gate would also shout if any of the dogs turned round. When I got on the trailer, there were loads of ropes. Then I took a couple of good ones, jumped off the trailer and ran as fast as I could, throwing the ropes over the fence while I was running. I then jumped for the top of the fence and got my arse out of the way. It was hard but it gave you a huge adrenalin rush when you got back over the fence. On the way home, we hatched a plan to go to the electrical store the next night as it was getting late by now. The plan sounded foolproof and we were all thinking of what stuff we'd like and who would have first pick.

The day after, we all met in the park and all the lads laughed about it and talked about what we were going to do. It was like a bullion robbery to us lot, so we needed to plan it out properly. Now, we were just waiting for the night-time to arrive, so we all went home to get our tea and arranged to meet at the pavilion in the top park at 7 pm. We all met up and started walking to the store. We were all full of great ideas and even talking about selling some stuff until we got outside when everyone started to have second thoughts.

"We're here now, so let's just see what it's like and if it's too hard, we'll go home," I said.

Anyway, it took us a good time to eventually get onto the roof and only half of us went up because the others had lost their bottle. We made our way across the roof, then all the brave soldiers started to shit themselves. We kicked the skylight in and waited a bit, then tied the rope to a steel chimney and dropped it down until it hit the floor; then they all started again with their bullshit, not wanting to go down the rope.

"I'm too heavy."

"I don't think I can make it down the rope."

"It's too high. I don't like heights."

"It's too fucking late now not to like heights as we're on the fucking roof," I said.

It was down to me to go in first.

"Give me the fucking rope," I said.

I don't know if you've ever gone down a rope, but I struggled like mad.

It was very hard to keep hold because the rope was burning my hand. I fell around 4 metres onto a shelf and the stuff went all over the place. I lay on the floor for a while in agony but they just shouted down, saying,

"What the fuck are you doing? Hurry up!"

I didn't answer them. I was really struggling as it had hurt me, so I stood up and got hold of the rope.

"You ok?" they shouted down.

"Yes, fucking great!" I said.

Then I tied this HiFi to the rope and they pulled it up. 'Great!' I thought, but then the fucking HiFi fell off the rope and broke into pieces when it hit the floor. Next, I tied some radios to the rope, and they got them to the roof; the rope came back, and I tied on the next couple of big radios and they started pulling them up – the idea was to get enough to have one each so we kept dropping the rope and putting on two more radios each time. Then, all of a sudden, all I could hear was police car sirens and the lads shouted down as they could see them coming from the roof. I tried to climb up the rope to get back out, but there was no way I could get up it. I just ran around like a headless chicken, thinking, 'What the fuck can I do now?' I looked for somewhere to hide then spotted a fire door in the corner with a little light over it, and I went over thinking I could hide behind the shelving, but then I pushed the bar of the door and it opened. 'Brilliant!' I thought. I still had to climb over the high spiked fence though. I climbed up and the spikes got my hands and jeans, then I jumped into the entry area at the rear of the houses and climbed over one of the walls. There was an old-style toilet at the bottom of the garden so I went in and locked the door and stayed there for a long time. I went out to the back gate a couple of times to listen out for the all-clear and then went and sat on the toilet again. After a while, the door opened and a big man was standing outside.

"What the fuck are you doing in there?" he said.

"I was going home and some boys chased me," I said and started to cry. "I ran and I climbed over the garden wall to hide from them and wait until they'd gone."

He could see I was scared.

"Come with me," he said.

He took me into his house and gave me a drink of juice.

"You poor thing; are you ok?" his wife said.

"I am now, but I was scared before!" I told her.

The man asked where I lived and I told him. He said his friend lived there and I said yes, he lives in the next street to me and I play with his son. The man then walked me across the road and waited at the bus stop with me, gave me 10 pence for the fare and put me on the bus. I thanked him and went home. I got back at 10.35 pm and my Mum screamed:

"Where the fuck have you been, you little shit?"

I said I'd been to the youth club and we just called at the chip shop on the way home.

"Get to bed before your dad gets in!" she said and gave me a slap round the face.

I went to lie on the bed I shared with my older brother but I couldn't get to sleep because I was still shaking, so I went and looked out of the window until he came in, then had to move as his bed was under the window. I went to bed just thinking how close I'd come to going to jail and thought I didn't want to do anything like that again. When I met all the lads the next day, they said they thought I'd been caught, so I told them the story and they said how lucky I was. They told me about how they'd all split up and had to get home through the golf course so as not to get caught.

"I think we need a little more preparation next time," I said.

Most of them laughed for the rest of the day about the fuck-ups and how everyone had got away. The strange thing was that one of the lads was in a toilet a couple of gardens away from where I was hiding. Two of us had got the bus home, but we'd come away with nothing. We'd left four belting radios on the roof and a floor full of damaged goods.

I did have a couple more bad days soon after that. I climbed over the back of the Co-op and took a load of flowers and bread that had been dropped off. When I went to school with these in my bag, one of the girls in my class said her mum worked there and she told her mum later. I was arrested and charged but was bound over. Then I broke into the school; I know it was a stupid thing to do, but I hated the place. I painted the headmaster's office and his windows black. I wouldn't have got caught if I hadn't written my name on his desk. So that was me done for criminal damage and they put the breaking and entering of the Co-op with it just to brighten my day.

That got me back to court, then because I'd been bound over for two years, I was charged with the trespassing and theft at the Co-op six months before as well. I ended up with two big fines and probation for two years. I had to pay £2 a week off my fine so I was doing everything I could to get that £2 because my Mum said there was no way she would pay anything, and if I missed a payment, there would be a warrant for my arrest and I would be sent down for six months. I didn't want that and I had no idea why I broke into the school, but the place had fucked me up in my younger life.

In all my younger years, I did everything I could for the old folks who lived near us and I would help them clear their rubbish away or just take their letters to the post box or go to the shop for them. Every time they offered me something I said no, thank you (because I'd already stolen some sweets from the shop), so I didn't need any more. Also, my parents had brought me up to respect the older folk and I used to love to listen to some of the stories old Mr Gilbert would tell me about when he was young because he had fought in both world wars. He was a lovely man, and his garden was awesome; it was very well looked after. Some of his stories about when he was young were mesmerising and funny too, and I adored him. One time, when I started walking home from his house, I saw The Beast from over the road and he shouted after me, but I just shouted back saying I had to go in and carried on running to my house. When I walked in, Mum said:

"What are you doing in?"

"Just changing my trainers," I said, but then I went and sat on the stairs.

I don't know why, but I felt safe sitting there as they were behind a door and no one went up the stairs until bedtime. All I could think of was killing The Beast across the road.

I think I was nearly 14 years old then, and I used to do odd jobs for people to earn money. An elderly lady, who was known as the Town Bike or Dirty Slut, asked me to block the side of her house to stop the kids and dogs going in, so it needed a gate and a fence to go along the grass.

"No problem. £30," I said.

"That's cheap," she said.

We went out that night and got a gate from the Posh Estate and then went over to the building site for timbers. Anyway, we got the job done a couple of days later and she was made up. She asked me if I would like a cup of tea and I said yes, so I went into the house with her and my mate Bob stayed outside. She asked me to go upstairs and get the cups from the back bedroom but when I went up and looked in the two bedrooms, I couldn't find any cups. Just then, she came up and pushed me onto the bed, then opened my shorts and started to blow me off. It was quite good as she had no teeth in. I understood why she got called a slut after this. She said she had only £20, and I just wanted to get out, so I accepted that and off I shot. She was about 56 years old. I told Bob and gave him £10.

"Such is life, mate," I told him.

I was surprised we got £20, to be truthful. I would still cut grass and cut hedges for old people free of charge out of respect for my elders and this was something I carried on through my younger life, from the small things like gardening and shopping to doing a lot of work for them as I got older, but I still couldn't charge. I got a better feeling doing it free. It was around this time that everyone on the estate was peeling shrimps to earn some money. The shrimp man would come and give you a huge 10kg bag of shrimps and you sat on the floor peeling them. Then you would put water in the bag to let them soak it up as it got you a little extra weight. Anyway, he used to come on a Tuesday to drop off and Thursday to collect and you got paid for the week before. I had got a bit pissed off with this bloke and when he was at the back of the van, I looked in the front and on the seat was a box of wage packets, so I thought if I just take a couple, he won't know; he will think he has forgotten them. So, I took two packets. I could have taken them all, but that would have been risky so the week after, I took two again, but one had £96 in and the other £75 so I had to hide the money and just pick at it. The third week I tried, and the bastard had locked the doors but his window was open a little so I just managed to reach one packet with £84 in it. I was going to the Bingo with my older sister, so I just bent down and picked it up and she thought someone had lost it so we split it, but when we got home, our kid wasn't happy. He said, "A bloke has worked all week for that. You have to give it back. You are out of order." Now, our kid may be bent but he does have morals so when we were in bed, my other brother was asleep and I told him how I had got it and he said, "Why didn't you say that?" and I said I couldn't because Mum would have taken it all off me. I offered him money for a drink and he said, "It's okay, I got paid today but thanks anyway."

I started to go and help my oldest brother's mate, SB, on his wagon to deliver all sorts from crisps to tampons and when we would stop to unload, I discovered a way to open a box of crisps without you noticing. At the bottom, I would rub my hand along the box a few times then take out what crisps I wanted and go to the next box. Now, he knew what I was doing but he was fine and if we could get anything that day, we would split it between us. Sometimes, you got stuff that shouldn't be on the trailer so you would cherry-pick. We were carrying beer too, but the only way of stealing this was to strip the pallet down to the base and there was always a case in the middle. You would put your second layer on top to catch the first and bridge the gap in the middle then build the pallet back up. It was hard work but it got me a case of beer to take home for my dad. When you got to your delivery point, they would strip the top three layers of the pallet down to see if any was missing but I had seen this before that's why I use to go to the bottom.

We had some great times, but he would go mad at me as I used to walk into the shop with boxes and if the owner was putting them away, I would walk out with something from another delivery person; it was like a game. At night, me and all the lads would go to this distribution company where they had around 300 to 400 wagons and most were loaded ready for the next day. They were loaded with everything you could think of that was sold inside a big supermarket. You would have to crawl round under the trailer to the back of each wagon to see if the doors were locked but around 10% of them weren't. Some were no good - we opened one and it was just full of pickled onions so you would lock that back up and carry on until you found one with a good mixture, i.e., pallets of beer and crisps and sweets. Then, we would make a long chain and pass the stuff along to the fence we had just come through and stack them on the other side. We normally took 2 cases of beer each as it was heavy and we had a long way to carry it. Sometimes we would stash stuff for the night after, or even the same night, and go back and take it closer to where we all used to sit but most of it was locked in someone's internal store. We would drink most, but whatever was left was kept for the next night.

When I was around 14/15, I was on the lane with all my mates, sitting on the benches as we use to do, talking and taking the piss. Next door to the off licence there was a clothes shop that sold sheepskin coats and it had already had the window broken and there was a huge 8x4 board nailed over the broken glass. All someone had done was break the window and take out what was on the dummy in the window and a couple of T-shirts folded on the floor. So, I said, "I bet we can get this board off." It took 4 of us to pull but we had to play-fight as the people next door kept looking through the curtains. All the lads stood outside and Klint came in with me. There was something blocking the door that leads to the window from inside so I put my back to it and pushed and it moved so we could get into the store. We started putting on clothes and jumpers so we could get out fully loaded, so I said to Klint, "You go first as your slower," and I watched him run across the road. Just as I was going to get out, a car pulled up outside and a man started to open the front gates, so I went back inside and panicked as he walked in. I was behind a shelf of T-shirts and jeans folded on the bottom and with jeans on hangers. Since he had put the lights on inside the shop, I could see just in front of me was a rack of jeans hanging down on hangers so I climbed inside the rack and put my back against the wall and my feet on the other side to press and lift my arse up so, I was half-floating inside the rack. All I wanted was to go to the toilet to empty my bowels. I was in panic mode, thinking should I just give myself up or see what happens, then, as I looked through the gaps, there were about 10 police officers in the shop and one walked back and started looking at the jeans that I was behind. I just kept thinking, 'Please fuck off; you're too fat for jeans.' Still, all I wanted was a shit and to be sick, but this policeman kept lifting the jeans and I could see his face so clearly and I thought he was going to grab me any minute now. By this time, the shop owner had phoned his wife and told her he was going to sleep in the shop until the next day. So how could I get out of there? Do I wait until someone comes into the shop tomorrow and roll out and join them, or wait till he is on his own and try to knock him out? My mind was racing and as time was getting on, I started to slide down the unit and by this time another couple of officers were looking at the jeans and his stock. I just wanted to roll out and lie on the floor as I was in agony. Anyway, the police said to the owner, "If I was you, I would go home; they won't come back." Then one of the officers got a call asking if the dogs were required. I felt sick again and I thought I am sure he must be able to smell the wind coming from my arse because I could, then the officers walked forward and I thought I was done for, but he said, "No, we don't need the dogs; we are just boarding up." Then the owner said, "It can't be kids because it took two of us some time to get this unit against the window-dressing door; not only that but there is float in the till and they haven't touched it." So, the officers helped put it back and fitted the board onto the window. When I heard all the cars leave, I got out and lay on the floor flat as I had been inside that unit for about 3 hours. I took a look round as I had loads of time but most of the stuff was for older people. I put on some T-shirts and a couple of jumpers and finished off with a cardigan. Then I went to the till, got it opened and took the float -about £28 - then I had to move the unit blocking the window-dresser's door and it took everything I had. I thought about the sheepskins, but the sign said Sheepskins Upstairs and I didn't have any of my keys with me and the door was locked and as this was off the cuff and not a planned robbery, I tried to get the door open and then thought I should just get out of there. I had luck on my side so I went into the window area and it took me some time to move this unit but I managed in the end and opened the door and stood inside the front window. I was looking up the road then trying to look the other way through the reflection of next door's bay window, when, all of a sudden, the curtains moved next door and I thought, 'Oh my god, she has seen me again. You have to go now!' So, I ran at the board and jumped up with both knees and my arms extended. The board came off completely and I ended up rolling in the main road. If a car had come along, I would have been killed. I ran across the road to the Public Toilets, took off all the clothes I had stolen and hung them on the back of the toilet door. Then I locked the toilet door, climbed over the top and ran through the allotments and across to the railway bridge and into the park. I hid in the bush at the entrance, looking both ways along the road and when it was clear, I sprinted across and then down the back entries of the terraced houses then across the field to my mate's flat. He lived on the top floor and I couldn't knock on the door as it was around 4 am, so I climbed up the balconies to the seventh floor and I knocked on his bedroom window. He opened the window and said, "Get in; be quiet!" Then he said, "I thought you had been caught; even all the lads said he isn't coming out of there." I asked him to get me a couple of rounds of bread and some water as I was drained so he came back with some cheese butties and a large glass of orange squash, and I told him all about everything that had happened inside the shop and he was gobsmacked. He said, "I thought you had no chance! I saw them all go in and I felt sick for you, then, when the van pulled up with the dogs in, the lads said 'let's fuck off; he is dead meat'. I thought they had taken the dogs in and you were locked up and then I was waiting for them to come for me." I said, "Don't be stupid. If they had taken me, no way would I have said you were with me, mate. We all have a code, and it can't be broken." The lady next door gave my description to the police so I did get a visit but because the police couldn't pin the shop on me, they brought back the suspended sentence I had got for robbing the Co-op and I had no idea. I was off school and out with my mates when this car pulled up and two guys got out. I knew one right away; he was 6'7" and his name was CID Kenny. We had crossed paths a few times so, they cuffed me, put me in the car and took me to the station then took me in and sat me on a bench and took the cuffs off and I was waiting for ages. Then, the back door opened and I could see into the rear yard so I thought I would nip out the back for a smoke and while I was there, no one came out, so I thought 'fuck it' and walked round the side to the bus stop and got on the bus and went to my mate's a couple of miles away from home. I sat in his house and told him what I had done, and he said, "You're nuts and playing the big man." It was just coming up to 6.45 pm and the youth club used to open at 7 pm so we went to the youth club and I was stood in the passageway waiting to go in. The next thing, a hand grabbed the back of my collar and dragged me out and down around 25 concrete steps, across the tarmac and threw me into the back of the car like a rag doll. All my mates were shouting but he just drove off and back to the station. I was put in a room with a cup of tea, and again it was taking ages because there was a huge fight in the station between two gangs and the police were struggling to control it. So off I went again, but it was after 10 pm when I got back to my mate's and they were going into town to the nightclub. So, I said, "Fuck it; my dad is on night shift and Mum thinks I am over the road at my mate's". Some of the lads I was with were dangerous and they spent most of the night just taking beer off people so, when it was time to leave, we walked home and when I was walking down the street, there was a car parked in front of my house, so I just went up to the car, opened the back door and it drove me to the station. This time, I was stripped and thrown in a cell but I got what I deserved really. They got me up at 7 am, charged me and then said, "You know how to get home, don't you?" Anyway, in court, I got 280 hours in Scrubs - not a nice place to be - and 280 hours community work. Scrubs was run by ex-sergeants from the police and the army and you went at the weekend and all they did was beat you with big sticks. The number of fights you got into was crazy, then, after you were done, they would beat both of you with the sticks. I was made up because I didn't win many fights so at least he was getting some punishment. My community hours started at an old folks' home in Prescott and it cost 12p on the bus so the first day in the office, a lady asked a lad how he got there. He said he got one bus into Old Swan then another bus from Old Swan to here and it cost 62p. She said, "Right, I will give you £1.24, that's your travel." Then she asked me, and I said I got a bus to St Helens then a bus from St Helens to Prescott. I said it cost me 85p, so she gave me £1.70 and we were all given our jobs to do. As we cleaned the floor, one of the lads said, "Have a look in that freezer - loads of ice creams and choc ices." So, I opened it up, gave everyone a choc ice and looked and there was a huge pack of bacon. Maybe I should have waited until I was going home but I thought, 'fuck it' and shoved it half down my pants and tied my coat arms around my waist. Anyway, as time got on, it was coming to going home time and she came out and said, Right, can you all put your stuff away and thank you for today. I will see you tomorrow - apart from YOU!" and pointed at me. She said, "In my office, now!" so I went in. She said, "One of the ladies who works here lives in your street, and it cost her 12p on the bus, so how did it cost you so much?" I said I wasn't at home; I was at my sisters in Parr. She wasn't too impressed and then said, "Also, what are you hiding down your pants?" and I said, "Nothing, miss," and she said, "The police station is two minutes away at the front or would you like to do it now?" I told her that one of the lads walked past and said, "You can have that," but she didn't believe it. She said, "Can you return the money I gave you? And leave - do not come back. I will ring your probation officer once you have left the building." So, that was me done; first day. I was gutted. When I got home, Mum asked how it was and I said, "Great, but I don't have to go tomorrow as they are breaking us up into teams." Next thing was a letter from my probation officer telling me to go in for another visit to see him and sort my next location. I told him the same story but he said, "I don't care but your next move will be Strangeways Prison." Then he sent me to Prescott Leisure Centre to do my hours. Anyway, the place wasn't open, so, I ended up at Scotch Barn Swimming Baths but had to do Saturday and Sunday morning and they had me cleaning the large café/bar upstairs the morning after someone had had a party. This one I did well and the boss loved me. I used to get food and all sorts from behind the bar; crisps, nuts, beer, cigars and sometimes you would come across cash. I would clean all the tables and pick up packs of cigarettes people had left and take stuff to the bin and whatever I was taking home, I would leave in a bin bag at the side of the bin, then just watch people swimming. The boss came in and asked if I was done and I said, "Nearly". He told me to go down and have a sauna when I was finished – it was great. It was even better when there had been no party; I just had to hoover. I would pack some bottles into a black bag to take home, and sometimes I found lost property and it was like Christmas - a nice watch, gold chain, trainers, shorts, T-shirts and training bags with clothes in, so, I would kit myself out then pack the rest in a bag to take home; it was easy. I would always take around 12 cans of pop and put them in the pantry at home as we didn't have a fridge when I was growing up. We only had a black and white tv and we used to warm the water up in the twin tub washing machine for a bath on a Sunday. When I was younger, you got in the bath in order, the oldest first.

    I had made a big knife and kept it hidden in the little coal cupboard at the side of the house. It was November and I saw The Beast going out, so I got the knife and followed him. He walked up the road to the pub and on each side of the road was a field, so I was walking up the field and there were gaps to go onto the path. I was sweating like mad, and each time, I kept thinking, 'go through the next gap and drive it into his neck', but it was getting harder and harder the further we got up the road and as we got to the top, I was still standing in the field with the knife and he was in the pub. I did think of sitting there until he was coming home but I just went back home, put the knife away and went down the street to my friends.

    You may think I have not mentioned anything about girlfriends, but take it from me, I was a pretty boy; I had my fair share and when I got a bit older,

I was doing at least one or two a week once I started to go to nightclubs at 15. I was taking them outside and doing them in the entry or car park. I was shocking; I had no morals. There was a guy in our street who had a video game. Now, we had nothing like that and he used to let us in so one night, me and my mate knocked on the door but he was at work. His wife said, "Come in! I will put the game on for you", and my mate said, "I am going to have to go", so I sat on the floor and she had a glass of wine. Then she came over and she sat at the side of me and put her hand on my privates. I didn't care as I was playing with the game. She then took it out and put her mouth on it then she pushed me back, took off her tights and had sex with me. I realised it was 10.30 pm and my dad would be home, so I had to pull out and cross over and go home. Dad asked where I had been so I said I was in Stew's playing with his video game with my mate. I asked if I could go back, and he said, "No, too late; you will have to go tomorrow".

I used to help a guy on a lorry doing deliveries all over the country. We delivered everything! He even let me drive the lorry and we had a good laugh every time we went out. Most times we would stop, and he would get breakfast and a brew, and we would sit there just taking the piss out of each other and one morning I told him all about the old woman taking her teeth out and he split his sides. He said even he wouldn't go near it; she was dirty in both ways and everyone had had her, so, he took the piss all day and when we got home. Still, I had loads of stuff - trays of Tic Tacs, cheese spread and sweets. This was a Friday; I will never forget because he said, "Do you fancy coming to Carlisle tomorrow?" I said it was no problem. He said, "I'll get you about 7.30 am." Anyway, the next day, he was still drunk from the night before! He got the wagon, pulled over in Ashton before the M6 and said, "Mate, you will have to drive". Now, I had driven the wagon around the car parks and around big places but never on the road but I had driven loads of cars, so we swapped seats and at 15 years old, I turned left onto the M6. I felt like a king! It was unreal. I did everything right; I indicated to come out and flashed people who let me in while he was asleep on the double seat on my left. When we came to our turn off, I woke him up and he said, "Go round this ring road and pull over." We swapped over and then pulled off. Only a few hundred metres further on there is another ring road and we got through that one and as we went through, there must have been 20 police cars pulling cars and vans over to the left-hand side. We just drove past and he said, "Bet you're glad we swapped over now, pal, or we would both be in jail; that was very close." I said, "I better not drive back", and he said, "I am okay now, mate. Let's get this drop done and go for a butty and a coffee." I said, "You could tell a hundred people what just happened, and no one would believe you." He said, "Better not to tell anyone, or we will both get into trouble."

Then came a huge day when I got into trouble at school. We broke into the storeroom, stole two javelins and a shotput and put them on the changing room roof. I have no idea why but that night, we went back and threw the javelins to each other, trying to catch them. Then, when we had had enough, we threw them through the headmaster's window and they stuck in his unit doors. The day after, I was in class and the headmaster came in, red-faced, big bloke, pointed at me and said, "You boy, my office, now!" So, I walked in front of him and when we got to his office, he threw me around the room, got me by the throat and lifted me up and said, "Finally, you are gone from my school, you horrible little prick! Now, fuck off home! I will not give you a letter to give to your dad, whom I know is a nice man. I will bring the letter to your house. Now, get out and off the school premises!" So, I walked home, and I was trying to think what shift my dad was on or if I could smooth Mum over; my head was in bits. When I got home, my dad was standing at the gate and as I walked in, he grabbed me and threw me down the steps then dragged me into the house. I was trying to lie but Dad hated people who lied, and he hit me a couple more times. Mum said that's enough, and I was told to strip off. I thought he was going to kill me! He punched me around the room but I did deserve it; then he said, "Now go upstairs!" I sat on my bed crying; not because of the beating but because I had let my dad down. Mum had no time for us but when Dad was on a day off, he would talk to you and ask what you had been up to and I had thrown that away. The next day, I got up and went into the front garden and dug it up, turned it over and raked it. I weeded the paths then started the back garden. Dad loved his garden and this was the only way back, so each day when I finished, I would water the plants and his vegetables and tomatoes, then have a shower in cold water in the back garden, get dried and go in the house and go to bed. This went on for a couple of weeks until one day, I was in the greenhouse and Dad came in. I was just watering the plants and he said, "They look ready for picking, lad". I asked which ones and he said, "These ones," and took about 6 tomatoes off the plants. He went into the house, washed them and cut them up and came outside with the tomatoes and some salt. He said, "Try one," and I did and said, "I don't like them; they taste strange." He said, "That's fresh fruit, lad; nothing better than your own fresh fruit." Then he picked a couple of lettuces out of the small boxes with plastic lids and walked in and shouted Mum to make him a salad butty. I just carried on outside, finished the grass and weeded the borders where he was growing plants and when he came out, he said, "We are going to have to cut these privets, lad." Fuck me, they were 8 foot tall and 70 foot long! I hated it but had to do my bit so the next day, I was on top of the privets, which turned into prickly bushes, kneeling on a plank cutting in front of me. It was awful, but we cut one side then we had to do the other. It was just after 6 pm when he said, "Well done, lad. That looks great. Get cleaned up and go out with your friends." The first thing we did was go over to the Posh Estate and get some gardening tools - one lawnmower and a set of electric hedge-cutters. The problem was then getting them to Dad. He was honest as the day he was born, so since my older brother was working for another brother's building company, I asked him if he would come home in the works van and just deliver them as Dad would not question anything he brought as they worked on loads of empty houses. The next day, Dad was made up; My brother told him they had been working on an empty house and the tools had been left in the garage, then he moved them into Dad's shed.

All my mates were out again at the weekend and we came across some nice gardening tools - a delving spade, some border scissors, border cutters and a big grass rake and I took two deckchairs as they hooked onto the back of the stuff I had over my shoulder. Again, I put all the tools in the shed and asked our kid that if Dad said anything, he was to tell him they were from another building job and he said it was okay but this would be the last time.

I said, "We need a big hose pipe," and he said, "I will get that from work." Dad was made up; he had all the gardening tools he needed. I wished I had the money to buy them and have money to get him what he wanted instead of watching him work 9 shifts with 2 days off. It was a hard job and it was killing him slowly. It's hard to write about someone you loved, and you will only understand when they have gone.

Then it was time for me to get a job. I had been doing weekends for my brother but because I had been to court twice, he would not give me a full-time job even though I had worked weekends since I was 12 years old; he was a wanker.

I went to a company called WHITES who had a site five minutes up the road building new bungalows so I was the can lad at £25 a week and had to pay Mum £15. I did not get any butties for work so my only survival was to go the shop and get the odd bits of change and buy something or one of the older guys would ask if I had no dinner and I would say, "Mum won't let me have any," and each would give me a butty. As I started to be trusted, I used to lock up the site and one day when I got home, my oldest brother said, "What's on your site?" When I said we had everything, he said, "Sort me some nails and a wheelbarrow." So next day, I locked up, put a box of 2-inch and a box of 4-inch nails into the new wheelbarrow and walked home with it. He picked them up that night and asked, "Is there any tie wires?" and I said, "Loads", so next day, I got two bundles of tie wires and a few packs of crocodile clips and a few boxes of screws, put them into another wheelbarrow and walked home. He was buzzing with me but still didn't give me any money. Then he asked if we had any Catnic lintels. I said, "Why don't you come tomorrow after 5.30 pm? The site shuts at 4-30 pm so it will be clear." He sent my brother in his place and we loaded about 10 of these lintels onto the van along with some drainage pipes and a couple of packs of collars, some pipe grease/glue and a box of work gloves. Then off he went so I locked up and took some gloves home for Dad for the garden. I got into work the next day and the boss called me into the office and said, "Listen, Chuck, (that's what they called me) there is loads of stuff missing off the site. Have you seen anyone as you are last to leave?" and I said, "By the time I have locked the containers and the cabins and walked back through, everyone has normally left." He said, "Tonight I want you to close my cabin, put the board on the window and you can still see through the holes; watch everyone and let's see which one of them are stealing from us." I said, "Boss, it will be 7 pm by the time I lock up and get home," so he gave me £10 out of petty cash and said, "This is overtime; let's get these twats. I will leave as normal because they won't do anything while I am on site and you write everything on that pad."

After he left, I wrote 'Dave and Mike in container but didn't come out with anything'. Then I walked round, locked up and I was away for 4-45 pm with £10. The next morning, he said, "Well done, Chuck. They must have known that you were staying because nothing has gone. Do you fancy doing it a couple of nights a week?" So, I said, "Yes, no problem. I will get the bastard one way or another." So, I was getting £20 a week extra for trying to spot myself stealing from the site. A few weeks later, we needed some wood at home as our kid was going to build a new shed for Dad. So, I put 20 x 8-foot 3x2 inch timbers on a wheelbarrow and tied them on then walked home with it. Dad asked who it was from, so I said, "My boss, Dave, said if I needed timber, to wait till they had gone home and take it, but I had to use the wheelbarrow. I will take it back tomorrow." I just put it in the old shed for Dad to use.

The odd time, there would be some people working on the drains or brickwork and the week after, they would get moved to another site and they would end up leaving their work clothes, coats or boots on site so I would fold them up and put them in a bag and put their name on the bag so it looked like I gave a shit. Then I would put them in the big cabin for a couple of weeks to make sure they didn't come back. Once I was sure, I would take them home and wash them. If there were jeans, I would take them up to fit me and some of the T-shirts and jumpers came up great so I used to wear them for going out in at night time. It was rare you would get a pair of boots that was your size, but you did get them and if someone left their trainers in the cabin and they were my size, I would take them home and wash them.

I had been driving since I was about 13 years old. We used to take old cars and have a ride round and then park them back up so they didn't miss them. I had a big bunch of keys so we would try loads and when one fitted, we were off for a drive around the estate and sometimes over the fields like a rally car. We had a good laugh, then, after we had finished, we would park it back in the same spot. The Christmas before I was 16, all the lads decided to go into town on the Mad Friday (it's the last working day for people and they all go and get pissed), so about 10 of us said, "Yes, I am in," but I didn't look old enough. A few more dropped out but about 5 ended up going, including my close friend, Alan, whom I looked on like a brother. Anyway, they had a great time and the plan was we were all meeting them at a party at 8 pm at a friend's house so I walked down to the benches where we all used to meet and there was only one person there. I said, "Have they all gone in front?" and he said, "No, there was a problem." I thought they had got drunk and started fighting but he then said they had got into most of the bars and they left at tea time to come home and meet us but the quickest way to walk was along the railway tracks. We had all done this hundreds of times and he said with it being dark, a train came and they all moved over and Alan said, "My foot is stuck!" The lads thought he was joking but he wasn't and couldn't make it out of the way. He was killed instantly in front of all his friends. I felt sick and sat on the bench and cried. I had been with him the day before. He was one of the jokers but he would always back you up. I didn't go to town with them as I know I would not have got into the pubs but maybe I would have done something; who knows? I went home and went to bed. It was a couple of days before Christmas and a nice young man had gone. I bet the lads who went with Alan for a drink were going through hell but I couldn't call them and when it all settled down, we never spoke about it just out of respect for Alan because he didn't deserve anything like that. All of his family went through hell that Christmas and so did a lot of the lads, but his family are still going through the same thing every Christmas and it will never change for them. It has been over 40 years but we will never forget Alan.

When I was 16, I bought an old Austin car and I took the lads out for the day. There were 8 of us in the car and about 40 cans of beer; God knows what was going through my head! We were out for hours, pulling up beside the girls in a shitty old Austin thinking I was cool. On Saturday nights, and we used to go from pub to pub so we were all pissed. One night, I dropped all my mates off and thought I would drive round for a bit longer; I was very drunk. I drove round the estate and one of the older guys out of the pub was walking along and I pulled over and shouted, "Vinny, do you want a lift home?" and he said, "No, pal, I am close enough but thanks," so I sped off and went down the hill, didn't stop at the T junction, went straight across and hit a lamp post. When I came to, I thought, 'I need to get out of here', so I reversed the car off and then started to drive it away. There was a loud scraping noise but I just needed to get it away, so I took it to a place where people used to park cars, then I left it, doors unlocked, and walked home. Next day, I was in work, so I used one of the office phones to report it missing. They asked when I had seen it last, and I said, "Last night outside my house. I had only bought it on Saturday and when I got up for work on Sunday, it had gone." They asked, "Why did you buy the car when you're only 16?" I said, "I was doing it up for when I was ready to drive." They said, "Did you insure the car?" and I said, "No, because I only got it yesterday". They swallowed the story and later on contacted me to say they had found the car, but it was not in a good condition. I said, "Don't say that! I have not paid for it yet and it's not insured!" Anyway, they told me where it was and I got a guy to pick it up for me and take it to his house. He told me that the passenger front wheel was stuck on the passenger front seat, so we decided to get it scrapped, but it was a good job Vinny hadn't taken a lift or he would have lost his leg or both legs; that was a strong lesson learned for me.

I was just over 17 and I had been driving for a few years and, being a smart arse, I thought I would go in for my driving test. So, at the club we use to drink in, I asked the woman who worked behind the bar to lend me her car on the Monday as I had been let down and I was picking something up for my dad. I couldn't say it was to take my test in as she would have known I didn't have a licence, so, after a few drinks and buying her a couple of drinks, I said I would only be about one hour and I would fill it with fuel, so she agreed. On the Monday morning, my test was at 11am so I went to her house, picked the car up, drove to the test centre, parked up and went inside. I sat in the waiting room with another 3 people and their driving instructors. The examiners came out and shouted each person apart from me, then this little fat bald bloke with a red nose came out and shouted my name. said he asked, "Where is your instructor?" and I said, "He has gone outside". I took him over to the Nissan Sunny and got into the car. He got in, sat down and said, "Does this have road tax and an MOT?" and I said, "Course it does". He tried to fasten his seatbelt but couldn't get it to clip in, so he said if the seatbelt didn't work, we would have to cancel the test, so he got out and walked back into the building. When I looked inside, I realised there was one of those rings off a keyring stuck inside so I pushed the key through it and got it out, tried the belt and it worked so I walked over and got him back out. He got in, put the seatbelt on and told me to reverse back and get to the entrance gate and turn left. So, I indicated, held the handbrake on, then, when it was clear, I pulled out. said he told me to go to the top of the hill, then there was a couple of small crossroads that I had to go over. Then he said, "Pull over on the left," so I indicated and pulled up and put my handbrake on. He then said, "I want you to turn the car round in the road doing a three-point turn," so I checked for traffic and did my three-point turn. said he then told me to drive back to the test centre and park up. When I looked down, he had taken his seatbelt off, so I asked him why and he said, "I am making sure it is working but it won't clip back in." So, I said, "It was fine before; why the fuck would you take it out before we got back?" He managed to clip it back in then I turned right and parked up and thought 'fuck me, that was easy' then he said, "Sorry to tell you, but you have failed your test and will have to re-book it." I lost it and said, "We have not done anything! All you have done is piss about with the seatbelt!" He was struggling to get out and I didn't see what he was doing as he had a clipboard and other papers on his knee and when he lifted his hand, I thought he was going to give me a smack, so I reacted and punched him in the face. Once he managed to get out, I stood outside saying, "Sorry, but I thought you was going for me; it was just a reaction." I sat in the car for a bit then thought, 'fuck it, just go home'. But as I drove out, two police cars blocked me in and got me out of the car. One asked, "Now. have we just passed our test?" and I said, "Yes, mate". He got hold of me and threw me on his bonnet then put the cuffs on and put me in his car and took me to the police station. He took me in, stripped me and put me in cell 12 so I was staying inside, and I was looking at a charge of ABH, stealing the car, no insurance, unaccompanied driving and no licence. They hit me with everything; the ABH, that is Actual Bodily Harm, was dropped in court as it was my word against his. I said I was just trying to get his seatbelt out as it was stuck, and it came out when I pulled it. My solicitor was shite; he wanted me to take a 6-month sentence and I said, "Are you fuckin' joking? You're here to help me." I ended up with another 8 points, but I already had 10 so I lost my licence and got fined £180 so really, I came off lightly but I did have a letter saying I was due to start work that week with my oldest brother in his building company, so they took that into consideration and that was what kept me out of jail. I told the lady who had leant me the car to say I had taken it and she didn't know, or she would have got the same fine as me. I know this as it had happened before when I was 16. I borrowed my mate's car to nip home for some more tools and I got pulled and was given a producer to take all my stuff to the police station. The bloke told them he had leant me the car because he thought I was fully covered but he got the same fine as I did.

I then got a job as an apprenticed plasterer with my brother and he was a wanker to work for; he paid £40 a week and I had to pay Mum £20. It didn't take me long to master plastering and I started to enjoy it. We were on a job where we had to knock the plaster off the full house back to brick damp course then we had to render all the walls in sand and cement and as I put the first mix on, my brother said, "I don't feel well. I am going home. Clean the mixer and walk home". But I thought, 'you know what? I have mixed this and I have got this.'

It was strange; it was a nice day and I just walked home. It was about 5 miles away, but I didn't care because I had just plastered my first walls and I had felt great. When I got home, Mum made me get undressed outside and I had to have a shower under the hose pipe in the garden, but I didn't care; this was normal for me. Next day, I walked to his house for 8.30 am and stood outside. He came out and got in the van and drove to the job. He opened the door and walked round and said, "Who did you get in?" and I told him I had done it myself as I didn't want to waste the mix. I thought I may as well use it, so I ended up rendering all the ground-floor walls, even the kitchen extension, then I cleaned up and walked home. He came over and kissed me on the head and said, "Let's go and get some finish, pal". On the way there, he said, "You know this finish is £3.50 a bag and we need 8 bags; see what you can do. "So, he pulled up and I put 8 bags into the van, walked inside the main shop to get two cups of coffee and walked back out to the van., When we finished the coffee and drove out, he said, "Give me the receipt, mate. How many did you book?" I said, "What receipt? I went for coffee - I thought you were booking them!" He said, "Mate, you are like owning a fucking money tree!" I asked if it got me a bonus and he said, "Your work and profit get the bonus." However, at the end of the week, he paid me £40 so I thought, 'fuck you' and everything I went to pick up, I booked and gave him the receipt. He said, "Come on, mate, you must be able to get something," and I said, "I am working to finish the job to get the bonus".

One of my last jobs with him was on a 4-storey house. We were to knock all the render off the side and re-render in a Tyrolean finish, like white, dotted, rough finish. When we got to rendering, he would say, "I will go and get us a sandwich" around 11am and not return, so I ended up doing 80% of the house. Then it was time to get the Tyrolean; this was £15.99 a bag plus VAT and we needed 12 bags. He said, "I will give you £5 cash for any bag you can steal", so I backed the van into the plaster shed and put in 12 bags of Tyrolean and drove out. Because he was in the pub the day before, he had not picked up the Tyrolean gun from the hire shop, which only opened at 9 am, so we got this and started on the top section. What you do is mix it very wet and brush it on the wall then mix it like cream, pour it into the gun and turn the handle and all these metal prongs would flick small dots onto the wall. It looked good, but it was a killer on your arms. So, then he said, "What sandwich do you want?" I thought he wouldn't be long because when you start this, you can't stop. Anyway, around 7.30 pm, one of my other brothers came and I had almost finished so he helped me clean up and took me to the pub where my brother had been all day. He was saying, "Here's my boy; people would pay good money to have my boy." I asked for my wages and he gave me £60, and I said, "Is that for the Tyrolean or my wage?" and he said, "Come on, mate, you have got £20 extra!" I said, "Yes, I know, but it's Saturday and I have worked 13 hours." He said, "I will sort you some extra next week too", but I said, "Save it, mate; shove it. You have been in here since dinner time; get yourself another prick to do your shit work!" I walked home and went for a drink in the lane with my friend but I was not happy at all. However, I had got rid of the greedy bastard I was working with who was only interested in making himself money and letting me do all the work. He rang me about 9 pm and said, "Come back to the pub and I will give you another £50." I said, "Mate, shove it up your arse I do not want anything to do with you anymore. You are one greedy lazy twat, now do me a favour and fuck off."

Later on, I got a job in Southport; a long way, but it was half-decent money plastering some new flats. All I was doing was skimming; it was easy. He had other blokes boarding the ceilings and walls and the ceilings were Artex, so we only plastered the walls.

By this time, I was getting close to 18 years old, and I was looking at buying my first house. I had been doing loads of private work for myself and getting all the plaster from work, so it was pure profit. I started hiding my money under the floorboards in the bedroom. By now, I was paying £40 a week board and still only got my tea. One night, we were all in the local village where all the shops were next to each other and there was around 25 to 30 of us so we said, "Let's mass the off-licence", and one of the lads said, "They know us all and the cameras are on". I told them that the substation at the end of my mate's street must feed all those shops, so after a lot of talking, it was down to me. I cut the lock on the gate and we had people spaced out along the main road so we knew what was going on. We left 10 people near the shop to run in when all the power went off. There were 4 big transformers buzzing like fuck, so, I cut the lock off one and pulled the lever over and said, "Is that it?" When they said no, I cut the next one, pulled the lever and asked the question again. Then, when the same answer came back, I thought, 'you know what - fuck it'. I cut the last two and pulled both levers and when we all ran out, every light in the area was off, all the houses, everything, apart from this one row of shops. So, I said, "Fuck it - hats on - let's pile in". What this meant was that everyone would start to fight with each other and while they were breaking it up, the others would get what they could then we all left before the Police came. We walked into the park to divide our gains up and spent most the night in the park. Next day, we went to the private club round the corner from the youth club and went below into the underground garage where they had an area fenced off with a metal fence. There were barrels of beer in there, so we climbed over, and all were empty apart from one. It was a big fucker, so we had to get it over the fence then over the outside wall and we took it to the back of the youth club. We wondered how the fuck we open this and someone said the top unscrews so a lad got a flat screwdriver and a hammer, and we started to tap it round to open it. Then someone said, "There is pressure in there; it will take your head off", so we started to press the top in but there was no pressure. We opened the top and then tried to pour it out into plastic cups. We spilled loads and it was fucking awful; the beer had gone off, but we all looked at each other and asked, "What's the worst thing that can happen?" One lad said, "You get the shits", so we all drank what was in the barrel; there was slime coming out, but we just flicked it out of the cups.

Later on, I had a few girls, but they were a pain. I remember it was a bank holiday and on the Sunday night, we all went to town and as we walked from one pub to another, there were 3 girls, all pissed. One was being sick and her mates had left her behind and I sat on the wall with her. She was very pretty so I asked her if she was okay. She said, "Why are you so nice?" I said I would take her to her mates or get her a cab home. She had her arms round me and she kept touching me and then she unbuttoned my pants. I offered to get her some water but then she felt sick again so I was rubbing her back. Next thing she said, "You are so kind; let me kiss you". I said no and she unzipped my pants. Next thing, I was having sex from behind; she kept standing up and holding my arms then she was sick again and I stopped. I said, "I can't do this". She was crying and begging me not to leave, so I got myself dressed and I sat on a bollard. Her friends came and asked what I was doing so I told them I hadn't touched her, but that they had left her alone and now they needed to get her home and I walked off. When I caught up to my mates, they said, "You don't need to say fuck all. We know you were going to do her". I said I was trying to help her but she started to undress me then Tez said it was a sick bowl she wanted not her back hole and we just laughed most of the night. When we got back to the club, there was a girl that I used to see when I was 12 years old. She was in the Labour Club with her mum. I hadn't seen her for 7 or 8 years. She was short, slim and very pretty. I was with the lads playing about and she kept looking over so I waved and asked if she would like a drink and she walked down to me and said, "Yes, please. It's nice to see you!" I asked where she had moved to and she said she was living with her sister so we chatted for a bit. After a bit, I said, "I can't hear you properly with the music", so we went outside and sat on the wall talking. I asked if she wanted to go for a walk so we walked over to the park and ended up having sex twice, then went back to the club. Tez said, "I got you two pints because you're a greedy bastard."

When I was 18, to keep me on the straight road, I started back playing rugby league and had some good times with the lads. Some of the games we use to play on the coach home were sick. For example, you pick a partner and put 50p in, then, when the whistle blows, whichever pair French-kissed longest took the pot. There were also bets to wank someone off or to give someone a gobble so me and GL used to clean up. GL would be my kissing partner - he would go down on me, then I would go down on him. It was all in good fun; we had a riot, and when we got back to home base, it got worse. You would end up sitting with no clothes on! Looking back, I can't remember many of the games I played in but I do remember a lot of the coach games, and what we use to get up to in the pub was crazy.

I won't forget when I was 18 and it was Christmas Eve; I was out with all the lads and I lived in a place where there were 7 pubs all within walking distance. There were even 4 within 100 metres of each other. Anyway, we were in the one halfway up the hill and this monster of a man used to come in. He was the town bully; he was a bodybuilder and he was a twat. We were all sat round a table and JP was sat in front of me and one of the lads came over and said something to JP. Next thing, JP jumped up and butted him and he hit the floor, so I pushed JP back to his seat. Then, this monster came over and demanded, "WHAT'S FUCKING GOING ON?" When no one took him on, he got hold of JP and said, "I ASKED YOU A QUESTION!" When I said, "What's it got to do with you? It's all sorted", he said to me, "SHUT UP, YOU LITTLE PRICK", then he hit me, and I hit the floor. I was then taken outside. He had split just above my lip on the left, so I walked the 50 metres to the other pub where my auntie worked. She was shocked and got ice and a cloth but I said, "Get me a pint; I am fine." Standing at the bar was a guy who I had said hello to in the past but didn't really know. We got talking and I found out he played Rugby Union and he knew about the bloke who had hit me. When I said I wanted to go back up to the first pub, he said I shouldn't. Despite this, I went back and as I got to the pub, there was a couple of lads fighting outside and one was JP, so I pulled them apart. Next thing, this monster came out and said, "I FUCKING TOLD YOU ONCE, LAD" and as I was going to say I was just breaking it up, he hit me then lifted me up and hit me again. Now my eye was swollen and I was bleeding from my nose, so I walked back to the other pub and my beer was still on the bar. As I picked it up, this guy said to me, "TOLD YOU SO" and we both laughed like fuck while my auntie patched me up; one to remember. Next day, my older brother came round. He kept shouting for me to come downstairs but I had only got home around 3am. I know, it was Christmas Day and I was in bed. Next thing I knew, he was in my room and when he saw me, he asked what I had been up to and I had to tell him. Turned out that the monster was our oldest brother's mate, so I was summoned to his place and he gave me a good hiding and said that the big guy would be in that pub on Wednesday night and I had to go to him and apologise for him hitting me! Anyway, I went into the pub and he was sat at the bar as he got free beer, so I walked over, ordered a drink and said, "Can you get these two chaps a drink?" He looked at me and said thanks and I said, "Sorry about the other night. I was trying to stop my mate", and he said, "It's okay, I spoke to your kid. I will watch your back from now on." I walked away and sat with my mates and they said, "Are you fucking stupid? You're lucky he didn't drop you again!" But I said, "No, it's all sorted now; he is okay". The guy I met in the bar that night now has his own pub and when I used to go in the odd time later in life, he would bring it up and say, "Tuck, tell these where me and you first met and had a drink together" and we just laugh about it. Mind you, he always says, "I give him his due; he had some balls going back".

The Beast across the road moved to a new house with the family. I had no idea where they had gone but I always said I would kill him as soon as I got chance.

Then, I started working for my brother's old partner and there were loads of us. My first job was in the mental hospital renovating one of the wards.

So, I went across the field to get to the job early and I waited outside near the skips. I had been there for ages when this guy came out and asked if I was okay. I said, "Yes, mate. I am just waiting for the lads", and he said, "Come on in. I am working on the same ward!" So, I followed him in and we went upstairs and into the big empty ward. He started telling me what we were doing and what walls we were taking down and I just walked round while he showed me. Next thing, a few of the builders came into the room and my brother said to me, "Are you ok?" and I said, "Yes, I am fine, why?" and he said, "That bloke is an inpatient and used to be a builder and wants to run this job! Don't worry, you will get use to them; loads come in through the day and some of them are sound". I shit myself and said, "How do they get out of the wards?" and he said, "They are let out; the bad ones are over the road in the high security units." When I asked if we would have to go there, he said, "Yes, but don't worry – there's always two of us." He started showing me the job and what to start doing so I started pulling the curtains down and taking them to the skip and after that I was working with all the lads. We had a great laugh every day. I loved it there! At the end of the ward, there was a big room and it was full of clothes. Fuck me, it was like going into Next and no one was serving! All day you could pick anything you wanted; jeans, T-shirts, sweatshirts, jumpers, trainers, even shoes, so I used to fold stuff up and put it in a binbag and leave it at the side of the skip so I could pick it up when I was walking home. As it started to get colder, I would get a couple of jumpers and a couple of coats out of the big patient dressing room. The best thing was that you could get clothes that were so good you could use them to go to the nightclub as they had some smart things. I got a lot of clothes from there and a couple of pairs of shoes and 4 pairs of trainers.

We worked at the mental hospital for about 14 months and we ended up doing jobs at different parts of the hospital but you got used to moving about most days.

We worked in all the hospitals and had a good laugh at them all, I would say, way too many to remember. I do remember it was summer and there was no rugby and we were all in the pub at 3 pm after work. We were still there at 8 pm - we had had a scream; it was a cracking pub! Anyway, our boss rang the pub and my brother went over as it was for him. He came back and said, "We have to go to Newton Hospital now; the drains are blocked". I told him to fuck off and he said, "You have to. There is only me and you". So, he drove about 10 miles to get to this hospital and he said, "It will be the same as last time; the drain is in the cellar". So, we got there and he was right. We got the manhole keys and he said, "I would take your boots, socks and pants off as that is over 900mm high". We had to wade about barefoot to find the manhole. Then you have to get the key in it so, as we were trying, all these floating shits are hitting me on my neck and my hair. My brother put his full head under and got the keys in after trying for ages and we got the lid off. Then I got the rods and started rodding. At last, we had 5-7 rods on with the pig's tail on the end and suddenly, all the water started to go and we were high -fiving each other while covered in human shit.

So, when all the water had gone, the full cellar floor was covered in shit, toilet paper and tampons. There was a fire hose on the wall so we had to hose the full cellar down and get it all down the drain. Then we hosed each other down, put the lid back and went back to van. We tried to get dry but everything was wet, so we put pants, socks and boots on and I asked him to drop me at the club near mine as I wanted to go and see the lads. I got a pint, drank it and went to the games room, but I stank so bad that I was thrown out of there. I went onto the dancefloor as my mate was dancing with his wife and he said, "What the fuck is that smell?" I said, "Oh, I have been doing the drains at the hospital", and he said, "Mate, go away!" Then two of the committee men came over and said, "Tuck, sorry mate, you're going to have to leave. You fucking stink and everyone is complaining about you." So, I agreed and called into the chip shop and ordered chips. The girl serving asked what the smell was and when I said it was my workpants, she asked me to wait outside so I sat on wall until she came out. When I got to the house, I asked Mum to pass some washing-up liquid out of the back window and I hooked the hose pipe up on the wall at 10.15 pm and had a cold shower outside. She made me throw my clothes away and when I got in the house, she sent me back out to shower again. Our kid picked me up at 8 am and the smell was still on both of us and you could taste it at the back of your throat. So, after work, we went for a pint then home for a very hot bath then bed for one hour and met the lads at 7 pm in the club.

We worked all over the hospital and in every ward from the kids to the mortuary. The bloke in the morgue was a great man to get on with so I used to go and sit with him when he was doing his work. He used to keep his sandwiches and milk in the fridge with the bodies in and he would rest his newspaper on their heads when having his break, but I got on great with him. One time, we were in the dispensary which was huge, and it was a drug addicts' paradise. I just took some paracetamol and ibuprofen and some plasters and spray skin. I had no idea what the other stuff was but a few of the lads helped themselves. We were working in the lead factory in Lancashire one time; it was like striking gold as you were surrounded by lead. We were told there were spot-checks on the way out, so we said 'okay'. We put a load on the back of the pick-up and covered it with sand and placed the mixer at the back and the bloke in the lodge was great; he came out and looked inside and on the back, then we drove off. One of the other lads had a crew cab and he had put the lead under the rear seat, and I thought, 'You prick; he only has to lift the black seat top up!' Anyway, we stored ours, me and our kid, then, as we started to work there a lot, the security changed on a weekend, so our kid went in as he was best at it. So, he arranged with the guard that we could fill a van for £100. So, I swapped my pick-up with one of the lads and took the van back. Once we had filled it and given him the money, we were black as hell but we took the load straight to the scrap yard and he gave us £410 for it, so, it was a good day. We hadn't done this for some time and our kid said, "Let's go back". So, we gave him another £100 and filled a van so much that we had to push it up the hill with the other van at the back of it, bumper to bumper, and we had to park it at my house as the scrapyard was closed. The morning after, we had to tow it up the hill then it was quite a flat run to the scrapyard, but when we got there, he was closed. We needed the van empty, so I said we should go to the other scrapyard. In total, there was 3.2 tons in a 1-ton van, and we got paid £660 and I said to our kid, "We have been getting ripped off for months", so we drove to the other scrapman and I don't know how our kid didn't kill him! He called him a greedy bastard and said, "You used to be a friend. That was a bigger load; we weighed in at 3 tons yesterday and got £410. You are a fucking arsehole!" His son, who was older than me, came out and our kid said, "If you don't go back in the house, I will fucking split you into two!" Both of them gave loads of excuses, saying it was bullshit that they had been ripping us off for months, but it didn't wash; they had done us, so our kid said they would get fuck all from now and we left. Then we went to another scrap man I had used before and got to know him. He was sound and even helped offload using a forklift truck, but he told us he knew where the lead had come from and could only take a couple of loads that size every week. The first scrapman kept phoning but our kid said we would never use him again just to let him know he had lost more than just our trust. After a few months, the security man was moved on to another site so we didn't have any more to sell.

On a Saturday, we would go up the pub early. The main Public Bar was closed but if we were with Big Bri, we could walk down through the back of the bar to get to the Public Bar and we would sit and play cards or play pool and we were filling our own glasses like we had always done. It was better when the old woman was on by herself and then you would have to start to hand them round. We all had about 4 pints each, three under the table or lined up along the floor below the bar; it was funny. One Saturday, someone said, "Fuck me, they have got a new tv" and the old guy said, "Yes, they put it in on Thursday". We had complained because we couldn't watch racing but you were not allowed to switch it on until 7 pm when the Public Bar main door was opened. Then, around 6.30 pm there was a knock on the window; it was Jim from near us. Now Jim was one hard man, so we went and opened the door and let him in. He asked if the landlord was in and I said no. He said, "Free ale? That's good because he barred me last week", and he had brought a huge plastic container to fill. I was crying laughing then he put his container in the doorway, drank two pints then pulled a stool out, stood on it, unplugged the tv, lifted it off the shelf and said, "Get that door, Tuck!" So, I opened the door and he said, "Put that beer on top of the tv, mate", then off he went. I walked back in and our kid said, "You should have dropped him off in the van", and I said, "No way am I getting involved, pal".

So, we all sat down playing cards. Next thing, the landlord came down, a little posh shit, and said, "Evening, gents", and he was whistling while he pulled a drink for a bloke and started to wash glasses. All of a sudden, he blew up; "WHERE THE FUCK IS MY TV?" We just looked at him and he said, "The lot of you! Get fucking out!" Big Bri looked over and said, "As soon as we have finished these drinks, John, we will all leave." John walked off, but the problem was there was still around 18 pints along the bar floor which we all had to get down us. But Bri said, "Leave all the glasses under this table," then we went to the club together, all in the pick-up truck, four in the front and 8 on the back. As we were driving through our estate, our kid was lifting the back up to tip and it was higher than the cab and a couple were lying at the tail gate covered in dust but it was a good laugh with good neighbours.

I did have a few friends who used to travel round the country doing all the post offices. I was surprised, but they had a good system of doing them too. They would go into a little town 4-5 hours away from where they lived and make sure it had a post office. Then, on the night they had chosen, they would go to the telegraph pole, remove the metal covering going up the side and cut through the cables with an axe, then re-fit the top metal cover so that every shop alarm would ring in the village or town. Then, they would sit in the pub watching the police fly round, then, when it went quiet, they would have a walk round until they had seen the BT vans had been called to fix the fault then they would go to the post office and get in through the back and take out the safe; they had hours to do this because there were no alarms working. They would end up getting it in the van and then they would wait until morning and drive out of the town when traffic was busy and make their way home, stopping off at their mate's farm and cutting the hinges off it and emptying the contents. Then, their mate would dump the safe for them in the canal. It was a really good set up and they kept out of town. Most times, they arranged it to coincide with a dentist's appointment. They would drop the dentist £100 to book the appointment, even giving them a card for the following visit, to prove you were at home on the day of the robbery.

Not long after, we worked on a cladding manufacturer's site and this place was full off rolls of aluminium. Most of the rolls were 50 metres long, about 600mm wide and they weighed around 180kg to 450kg. Each roll had its weight written on it so we had to be careful as the security man was hot on this site. So, our kid said, "What can you lift on your own?" and I said about 200kg so he said, "Right, we go in, he opens the gate and when he comes out, you hide in back and I will walk him inside to get my tool bag. I will leave it there; you will hear him as he coughs all the time." So, he got out and started talking to the guard. Next thing, they both went inside I opened both back doors and lifted one roll in then I looked through the window in the door and thought 'Fuck it' and went for another one. I lifted it but couldn't get it up the step, so it dropped on its side and I pushed it in and put dust sheets over the rolls. I could hear our kid as he was making bird noises so I jumped into the back of the van and got under the dust sheet covering the aluminium rolls. Then he came out, opened the van door, put his tools on the passenger seat and talked to the old guy for a bit. After a while, he opened the electric gate and we drove out. We drove half a mile away and our kid said, "You okay?" I said yes, stood up and lifted his tools into the back. He said, "What have you done?" I asked him what he meant and he told me my arms were bleeding because the rolls had sharp edges so he gave me some paper towel and off we went to our new scrapman. We parked up and let most people leave then I went in to see him. He asked, "What you got, kid?" I said, "Ali". He asked if I needed a bin, gave me a slip and the lad brought the bin out. When our kid opened the door, he lifted the dust sheet and said, "You fucking beauty, you got two! How the fuck did you lift this?" One roll weighed 340kg and the other was 260kg. When I went back to desk with the slip, he said, "I can only do one of these a week since I know where it is from," so I said, "No problem; there won't be a lot of this", and he paid us a lot of money, so we went home and celebrated.

We did do it another 4 or 5 times but had to break it up because our kid couldn't keep asking for his tools. Then we started a job at the cheese factory, taking walls out and doing the offices. was All the walls were covered in checker plate sheets of aluminium and I said to our kid that these were only fixed on with 4 screws, but he said, "Don't touch these. Just round the corner, there is a quarter of the plant that they don't use anymore. We will have a look in there." At the weekend, we were in and got our concrete job done. We had taken the security man some porn videos, so he was made up and we drove round to the other side of the site. It looked just like the other part where we were working but with no machines. So, our kid said, "What do you think?" I said, "Let's get one off and see what it is like to carry". The sheet was 8 feet by 4 feet, and it was around 300kg, so we struggled like mad as the van couldn't get into the building. Our kid said we needed a fork truck so I went off to look for one but could only find a pallet truck. We ended up clearing a full wall! There were around 12 sheets in the van, which was on its arse, and because we had another job to go to, we went straight to the scrapman who knew me and off-loaded. We got nearly £1400 each - it was awesome! I said, "We will go to your house, then mine, to drop the cash; just keep £100 in your pocket." When he asked why, I said, "I can't go into the other factory with this sticking out of my pants!" At the other factory, there were about 5 lads and we were doing a big repair inside. Next thing, our kid came over and said, "I will come out with you when you take the next dumper load out. I need to show you something", so I said, "No problem; jump on!" I drove through the factory and outside to dump the bucketload and our kid said, "Here, have a look at this!" It was a room full of hundreds of boxes of camping stoves and camping lights all with the can of gas in the box. So, I said, "I don't go camping," and he said, "Neither do I but they're going in the van!" So, we loaded about 30 boxes into the van. Then we walked to the side door of the warehouse and found it full of gas fires. I said, "Fuck me, I need a new fire," so we grabbed the catalogue of fires and chose one then walked round until we found them. I took one for home and one for my brother-in-law as we got on well. Our kid took a couple then said, "Put 10 more in; I will get rid of them today." I said, "You better had as we have to pick 2 of the lads up in the morning." When we got back, one of the lads came over to me and said, "Tuck, you have been up to no good, you wanker!" I said, "No, mate, but I will show you tomorrow", so that kept him happy. I only showed him the camping stuff and he said, "Wow! I can use these when I'm fishing." I told him to help himself and when he asked why I wasn't taking any, I just said, "I don't go camping or fishing so they are no good for me."

We finished work at around 3 pm and we were last to leave. We did have to give anyone a lift with us so I dropped mine off and then our kid drove off with all the rest. Then it was a night out with 8 friends and their wives. We used to go every Saturday night; we had a good laugh. One of my mates used to get me all sorts from where he worked so when we were alone, I said to Big C about the fires and he said, "Mate, if you can but don't get yourself in trouble". I loved this guy as we had grown up together, gone to the same schools and ended up in the same rugby club, so next day, I showed the lad the camping stuff and told our kid, "I need a fire for Big C", and he said, "No problems", so we went in and we had a good time in there, loaded what we needed and got a good few things to sell on.

One of the big lads, Davo, was a lick-arse and every time the boss would turn up, he would have a spade in his hand and then start to move sand. He did this all the time; if he was walking round, he would carry a 4-foot length of 3x2 just in case the boss come, then he would say, "I am just making some ground stakes". So, to get him back, I went into the cabin and there was a spider in the corner so I picked it up. It was about 85mm to 95mm spread out because they spread their legs when you pick them up. I got Davo's lunch box, took the lid off and took out the top sandwich. I put the spider on the sandwich and put the top back on the box and put it back in his bag. Then we hit dinner time but I didn't tell anyone because they would have told him. He sat down with his cup of tea, his newspaper on the table and his box at the side and he took the lid off the box. He picked up the wrong sandwich first, so I was sitting watching him and our kid said, "What you doing?" I just smiled. Then Davo took the one with the spider out and just read the paper and took a big bite. The leg of the spider was wiggling about out of the sandwich but he took another bite and finished the lot! I was dumbstruck and I only told our kid afterwards so he couldn't stop him eating it.

    A couple of weeks later, we got a contract with the brewery. This was around the same year when Health and Safety had just become really strict and our kid had to supply all his workers with hard hats and a high vis vest. He was well pissed off as he didn't like to spend money. At first, he tried to make us buy them and when we said no, because he had to have them for the new contract, he bought them for the 16 people who worked for him and he got everyone to sign to say he had given them to us. (He knew we wouldn't wear them but this was to protect him in case you got hurt.) Now, in the team we had Big Davo. He had the biggest head you have ever seen; he was a sniper's dream, but we couldn't get a hard hat to fit him. He was a big soft lump, 6' 5" and 22 stone and our kid gave him a hard hat with the XXXL high vis and said, "Make them fit you. I don't give a fuck how, just make them fit!" Our kid was a big man too, but athletic and played professional rugby, so you did what he said. We started our first brewery job and ended up renovating an off-licence in Sale, Manchester, so, along with the two women who worked there, we moved all the stock and fitted a big dust block, ceiling to floor in blue thick plastic, to save dust going into the other side. We sat down to eat our dinner on the floor and our kid kept sliding half bottles of whiskey across the floor to me. I was pissing myself laughing and one of the women said, "What you are doing back there?" and we said, "Just telling jokes, love!" I shoved about 800 cigarettes down my top and got three bottles of good whiskey for our kid. He was about 12 years older than me but you wouldn't think it; he was like a kid! He was laughing when I came back, so I said, "What have you done?" and he said, "You sounded like my milkman then when you were going outside." When I got back to my dinner, I was sitting on my coat and when I sat down, he just laughed. He had put two bottles of wine in each sleeve and said, "The wife likes that." Mine did too so we carried out a few cases. The women were more interested in protecting the sweets behind the counter. I walked round and asked for a Mars bar and she charged me for it! We were fitting an RSJ steel beam in so as we were getting the beam off the lifter, I said, "Let me get on the stairs to get a better hold. Now, keep hitting the beam while I go upstairs." He carried on hitting the beam. The women asked how long he was going to be doing that and he said, "Couple more just to fix it in place, love." Meanwhile, I brought three boxes of chocolates down - Mars, Crunchy and Ripple - and a few sleeves of cigarettes because she had pissed me off charging for the bar of chocolate. Both me and my other brother smoked back then so I split them with him and he was made up.

We had another very big RSJ to fit and it needed 12 men to do it as we had to knock a big hole in the side of the building and feed it through from outside. Our kid said, "The boss of the brewery is meeting me there so make sure you have your high vis and hard hats on or your walking home, and that's a promise."

So, we waited until our kid's car was at the traffic lights, then we all put them on and carried on. We had a fork truck outside holding the beam and all the pavement and some of the road had barriers round them. This was only to impress the brewery boss who turned up in a brand-new Range Rover. We had got everything ready and started to feed the beam through but our kid said, "Take it out and wait for him so he can see how professional we are." So, when this guy appeared, our kid started instructing us on how to fit it. I looked outside and our kid was with this big boss and talking shit; he made out as though he had been there all day and had overseen the job! The boss was very impressed - he shook our kid's hand and off he went, then our kid came in and said, "Well done!" Next thing, Big Davo walked round the corner and he had cut the bottom rim off the hard hat and cut lines up from the bottom, all done with a petrol whizzer, then he had put pipe lagging round the base and gaffer-taped the lagging to the hat so it would fit on his head! Our kid looked at him and said, "What the fuck have you done?" and Davo said, "You said make it fit!" Everyone was laughing like hell, even our kid, and he said, "If anyone from the brewery comes, make him take off that hat and high vis and stand him the other side of the counter so he looks like he is buying something or we will all get kicked off." So, as soon as our kid left, the hard hats and high vis came off, the brickwork got finished then we left site early.

We did a couple of weeks there then ended up working on the hospitals for a few months. I had had a lot of hospital surgery - both shoulders twice, a disc out of my neck and my right quad torn, then my left quad ripped. I then had two double hernia operations. For now, I had left my lower back and also the new left shoulder, as I was going to have some done when I got to 60 years old, but I was struggling all the time with my lower spine. It was even causing my left leg to give way and I had fallen downstairs a few times, but I said that I would put it off until I couldn't take any more of the pain. This was mostly in the morning, then, after you had got up and moved about, you started to loosen off and you could get on with your day.

then came the news that we were doing another off-licence in Bolton. We got there on the first day and were looking round and the boss from the brewery was in and he said, "Yes, the owner has done a midnight flit owing us around £40,000 plus whatever is missing, so we have a new manager coming in a couple of days and he will do a full stock check." Now, in the back room, there was a full height cupboard at either side of the chimney breast, I had opened the door and it was full top to bottom with sleeves of every brand of cigarettes you could think of, so I told the lad with me not to go near those cupboards, but when my boss walked in, this dickhead said, "Are these cupboards coming out?" My boss opened them and shouted the brewery boss and he counted everything that was in there! I went off my head. I wanted to smash his face in! I said, "What a fucking prick you are!" but he just looked at me. I said, "No one was going to open them so we could have taken the lot and the bloke who has left would have got the blame." He said, "Oh, I didn't think of that." After both bosses had left, he asked me what we were doing, and I said, "I am going down the cellar. I don't give a fuck what you do!" I had no idea about wine but I took 20 bottles and a load of sweets for my girl.

When we went back, our kid was with us. The new guy had arrived and he was a wanker – you couldn't get away with anything. Once more, the plastic dust barrier was put up, but he had left all the stock on the floor, so me and our kid passed sleeves of cigarettes and the odd bottle of spirits under the barrier. I think we did 4 weeks on there but we took our fair share.

I had, by this time, been out with my fair share of girls and one of them I thought was *the* one, so we started to save up together and we got engaged but I didn't tell any of my family. At the time I was with her, I was in a boy band with the lads and we used to put an act on at the end of the night and the pub was packed out every time we were on. It was great; there were about 12 of us in the band and we were well trained. We also had a couple of side acts and singing, but it broke up when the landlord, who didn't even give us a drink for doing it, wanted to charge one of the lads to have a party in the pub. Loads of the lads didn't go back, and I was one of them!

By this time, my dad was having time off work, and this wasn't like him. He never missed a day. He was only 52 and he even stopped going on nights out, but if I was home, we would talk to each other about work and he would always crack a sly dry joke and he made me laugh. He would always ask about my day and come back at me with some funny comment. Then, one night I was home early and we were watching snooker on TV and Jimmy White had just knocked a ball off about 6 cushions and into the corner pocket and Dad said "Jammy bugger!" This was odd because Dad never swore and didn't like people swearing, so I said, "That's me; do you want anything?" and he said, "Get me a glass of water, cock", so I brought the water and he said the same thing - "Goodnight; God bless". I went to bed then I was woken up by my Mum running downstairs and I thought that was strange. Next thing, she shouted me so I ran down, and Dad was on the floor on his back, struggling to breathe. We didn't know what to do! I just kept saying, "Don't fucking die on me, please don't die!" I ran over the road and got my brother-in-law out of bed. We both ran over to my home and he was still alive, and Mum was in the kitchen with him. I had hold of his head, pulling it back to keep his airway open and I said, "Don't you fucking leave me!" and all I could do was cry. We tried for about half an hour then Dad smiled at me and he was gone. The ambulance had just got there and some of my local family started turning up at the house. They were all crying. I walked out and walked up the road. It was about 3.30 am and I sat in the doorway of the church that was at the top of the hill; a nice small church and a nice priest. But the last thing I wanted in my life was to lose the most amazing man you could ever know. I sat in the doorway all night; I thought my world had ended. The man I totally worshipped had been taken away. Life didn't seem right - all these dropout shitbags who have never worked a day in their life getting out of bed at dinner time - they are all okay but my dad had been taken away. He worked all his life, he never disliked anyone and he always tried to help people. I was beginning to wonder if there was a God at all because what he had just done was not right. Later, I woke up in the church doorway and the old priest was standing over me. He had covered me with a blanket and he asked if I was okay. He helped me up and brushed all the dust off me and took me inside and made me a cup of tea and I told him what had happened. He said, "You have just told me your father was in pain but he is only young. I would say don't be selfish; if he is in pain, let him rest. That is why he smiled at you because his pain had gone away." I sat at the table crying but he said, "Tears will heal you, but understand, you may have lost your dad, but would you sooner he be in pain or at rest without pain? There is only one option." I said I wanted him without the pain and he said, "If that option was available, your dad would still be with us."

It killed me. I didn't care for life; I didn't sleep. I sat in the pub the next night with everyone saying sorry and telling me how wonderful he was, but I was angry at him because he had left me. I didn't get the chance to go to the pub for a drink with my dad like all my mates; it was fucking awful. It would upset me when lads came into the pub with their dad. There were alcoholics drinking every day and night, older than my dad, so why him and not one of these scumbags? The night before his funeral, I had been drinking with a couple of my mates. The pub was closing and my mates had gone home and there was just me and this alcoholic left in the bar so we both went out together and the door shut behind us. Then this pisshead said to me, "Your dad was a great man". I said, "How the fuck do you know?" and he said that he used to drink in the same pub. He tried to hug me but I lost it and knocked him out. I walked home and left him in the road.

It showed at his funeral how well liked my dad was because around 2000 people turned out at the crematorium. Afterwards, we went out with all my brothers and we got pissed. We were still out at 4 am. I didn't want to go home because I knew what was waiting for me; a horrible, twisted woman. She threw all of Dad's stuff out a couple of days after he had died and burned them along with all the pictures of him. She was twisted and she got pissed every night, so when I walked in and she stood up and said, "I AM THE FUCKING BOSS NOW", I got some work clothes, went through the front door and slept at my mate's house. I was struggling to cope with the woman, she was so horrible. All she was interested in was money! She said, "You will have to pay more money, that's all, or you will have to leave!" I was already paying £40 in 1983. I was really struggling to get over Dad. I couldn't get over how someone so young and nice could be taken away, yet all those pissheads in the pub got away without a day's work. I thought that if there was a God, he wasn't doing a great job. It took me a long time to get over that and I hated sleeping in the house where he had died, so I needed my own home.

. I carried on working hard. I was working until 11pm most nights, only because I didn't want to go home to Mum. I was working for a dentist in Liverpool, patching up their old plaster coves on the ceilings. Once I had done one, everybody these people knew wanted me to do work for them so I would bank some of the money I made from these jobs and would not tell anyone how much I had saved.

I then ended up meeting a girl who was quite nice looking but she was hard work; one of those girls who wanted all the time. I used to stay at her house because I hated it at home. I just went home to get some more clothes. I was still paying £40 a week for food I wasn't eating, but that's life. This girl had left her boyfriend to be with me and I thought she told me that she was single. I had been seeing her for some time now; it had its ups and downs and we had been saving up for 3 years when she said she wanted to go away with her mum. I said no problem, so paid the £800 for her to go and gave her £300 spending money. Anyway, she had come back home on the Saturday so I rang, and she said she was knackered after the flight, so I asked if she wanted me to ring her later and she told me to call about 7 pm and see how she felt. When I rang, her sister told me she was asleep so I decided to go out with the lads. Next day at work, one of the lads was asking me about her and I told him what had happened. He said I should go round there in the van after work, so I went straight to her house and her sister answered the door but kept it closed slightly. Eventually, she said, "I am going to have to tell you that she has met someone and has gone to see him." I said, "Thanks for being honest". I walked away, got in the van and drove off. I parked up and sat in the van crying, then after a bit, I pulled myself together and went to meet the lads in the pub for a Sunday afternoon pint. After I got home, had a sleep till 6 pm then had a cold shower under the hose pipe, I had something to eat and my mate picked me up at 6.55 pm and we got to the pub for 7 pm for a night out with the rugby lads. We would all get the bus to town, walk round, have a drink with lads from other teams and have a laugh and I thought, 'Fuck me, I have missed out on this for the past three years'.

I had booked a couple of days off work as I wanted to sort my money out of the account I had with the ex-girlfriend. I had put in £150 a week for close on 3 years and I thought there must be £18000 to £23000. Anyway, when I got the total, it was £400.50p. I was fucking fuming! I didn't want any contact with her, but I had to ring her mum's. She came on the phone and I said, "You are a fucking slut! What have *you* done with all the money *I* had saved in the bank?" and she came back crying saying we had both spent it on clothes and shoes! I said, "What fucking clothes and shoes?!" She said, "You had a shirt the other week and you have had underpants." I totally lost it! I said, "You fucking arsehole! You have spent everything I have work for, you BASTARD! I hope you fucking die, you bitch," and she just cried and I slammed the phone down. I had a couple of weeks of being glum and the lads helped me, and we started taking girls back home on a Saturday night so I soon forgot about her. Then, about 6 months after, I was driving down this main road and I saw her car coming towards me. I didn't take any notice at first, then she came onto *my* side of the road! I was in a pick-up truck, so I carried on, but it was me who had to turn off the road onto the pavement! She was nuts! Then the council was laying a damp course in our homes so I put a star lock on my bedroom and the next thing I got home and one of the blokes said, "Your girlfriend was here before. She needed something out of your room." So, I ran up, went into the room and took my bottom drawer out as my money was under the unit. Anyway, she hadn't touched it, but she had made my bed so I stripped it off to check it then later on, I rang her and said, "What the fuck are you playing at? I am going to call the police!" She said, "I just wanted those boxer shorts I bought you back as I wouldn't like another girl to see you in them." I said, "You are sick! You have a problem, you thick bitch, now leave me alone. You are not fucking right in the head! You have taken me for a ride for 3 years, you fucking slag, now fuck off away from me; I don't want to see you again!" I said all this even though it killed me inside. I had never suffered like this before. It was just like when I lost my dad, then I get this thrown at me! I didn't know what to do or who to turn to, so all I did was go to the pub every night. I was always last out and I didn't want to go home because Dad wasn't there. Then, the next day, I told one of my older sisters who went into her work, grabbed her round the neck and said, "You go in my mum's house again and I will fucking come here and kill you in front of your work friends!" After that, I didn't hear from her for about 6 months. then me and all the lads were in a pub and she walked in. I went over and saw she was on her own drinking coke. I had had a few drinks as we had played rugby that afternoon and as I was talking to her, the old guy I used to go on the wagon with said to me, "Keep clear, mate. She is dangerous". But I ended up in her car and going to the next pub where the rest of the team was. I walked in and they were all in the bar, but they could see me, so I went into the toilet. My cousin came in and said, "What the fuck are you doing with her, you are fucking idiot?" then slapped me hard round my face, knocking me down. I said we were just talking, so then he said, "I will give you 10 minutes to get rid then I will come in and kick you round the pub. She is a twat!" So, I went back and she asked what the mark on my face was and I said, "I was given that to remind me what you had done to me". She said she had better go and left and I went into the bar and my cousin said, "I don't want to see you go through that again; you don't deserve it." He gave me a hug; he was a big man too and a beast with it, but I knew he was on my side.

I will admit, this break-up nearly killed me. This was the first time I had really liked someone. I should have seen something when she bought herself an engagement ring but I trusted her. I had lost my dad and the girlfriend I trusted stripped me of 3 years' wages. It was a good job I kept my extra work money at home or that would have gone too, so, I just carried on with my work the best I could. I met a couple of girls along the way, but nothing took my fancy. Looking back, I wish I could have married someone from my council estate - you will understand later. I met a lovely girl; slim and pretty, from near me and she lived in a posh house. We used to go out at weekends and have a great time. She was the only girl I could have a laugh with - I have never been out with a girl who was fun too, but when she started to say she was falling in love with me, I backed off. I had panicked but that was one big mistake because she was great, but I didn't want to get hurt again and I let her go. Looking back, I know I fucked up – she was fantastic – lovely long curly hair and a great body, but because of my insecurity, I got scared it might happen again. I had lost all trust in women after the last one took me for a ride but it was a mistake I regretted for a long time.

I carried on working with my family and we had loads of contracts. One big job was at an old folk's home run by the church and nuns. Some were lovely; some were absolutely twats, but we had a great laugh.

Our kid had been routing round, as he does, and he was in the cellar and found hundreds of Crow Scarers. These are very loud bangers on a rope that burned slowly, so a two-metre rope with five on would last for roughly 3 hours. They used to put them in the fields to scare crows as it was louder than a shotgun. Anyway, we were working in this place and fitting new drainage in each room, then plastering the rooms so they could be decorated, but if you were in a room plastering and there was an open drainpipe coming through the ceiling or wall, these bastards would light the bangers and drop them through the pipe into your room. Fuck me, the noise was shocking! Your ears just buzzed for hours and you had no idea who it was. So, I went round to the brew cabin and they were about 20 minutes into their chips. I lit one, opened the door and threw it in. All you could hear was all the chairs and tables being pushed round as they tried to get out; it was funny.

I was buying myself a house in the local area and was just going through with the mortgage. I couldn't wait just to move away from Mum. Then I met a young girl. I was 21, she was 18. She was stunning and posh but she was lovely. We got on great. I was falling for her but had second thoughts as I had been burned before so I thought I would take it slow and we got on great. We had been seeing each other for about 3 months and she was lovely to get on with, very easy going and wasn't in your face all the time. She used to come and watch me play rugby and then she would go home and let me go out with the lads. Then I would meet her later and we would stay at my sister's house over the weekend. One day, she bought me a gift and gave me a card and it said 'I am falling in love with you!' When I opened her gift, it was some boxer shorts and my heart sank. I knew deep down she was the one for me but I wasn't ready for the 'I love you' part just yet, not after everything I had been through. I ended up not seeing her again and that hurt me more than anything. Even to this day now when I am writing this, she was 100% the one for me and I fucked up big time - she was amazing.

So, I got on with my life and started going out with the lads again at weekends. I ended up meeting a girl who worked behind the bar and we got on. She was a bit bossy but I was used to getting bossed by my Mum and at work by my brother so one more didn't make any difference. However, she said, "I don't want to live in the area where you're buying the house. It's full of scruffs. I want to live in Eccleston." I didn't think we could afford that so we got a cheap house in a nicer part of our area, so that made her happy. I renovated it all by myself. I took all the ceilings down, knocked all the plaster off and dug 2 foot out of the floors, then I dug a 22-foot extension on the back. It's fucking hard on your own trying to nip there through a workday to do a bit, then going after work at 4.30 pm and working till 11.30 pm, then going home and going back to work in the morning and starting all over again. It's a good job I was left alone at work or I would have been screwed as there would be no way I could keep going to my house to work on it. In the house, I dropped all the ceilings to 2020mm upstairs and downstairs, I mixed all my own sand and cement to plaster all the walls throughout the house, I took out both chimney breasts and the centre wall and got the bricklayer to build the shell of the kitchen and bathroom and also the porch and bay window. In return, I plastered his house for him. I got to the finishing part after two years of hard work. My mate fitted my carpet, and we got a three-piece suite from her relative. We had a nice gas fire and oven and hob I got from work, and the fridge I took out of one of the brew rooms at the gas fire factory. It just wanted a good clean. I got the kitchen from MFI. I put it all together and put all the units in place and her uncle fitted them in for me. My brother-in-law did the plumbing, with me and two of my mates doing the rewire first fix. I did the second fix myself. It took two years of non-stop hard work and cost me around £2000, but she didn't appreciate the effort that went into it.

Back then, I was only getting money from doing a lot of work as I had stopped breaking the law with my mates. I use to earn extra from work if we came across anything we could take and sell, but we all done that.

The girlfriend didn't do a thing; never came near the house, didn't bring me a drink or any food. She didn't give a fuck and I should have jumped out then because I was set for a rough life with her.

Two weeks after the house was finished, we got married. I still don't know why. Apart from her being pregnant, why the fuck did I get married? I always said I wouldn't get married after what I had been through with the one that ripped me off and even this one started great very loving, very loyal, but then started to question everything and complained about everything no matter what you did. If I had to go and do a job after work at 6 pm earning you £60, she complained. I had to work weekends; she complained. I was the only married man who did not get any sandwiches made for him for work by his wife. She was okay with the wage pack I used to give her and the extra money I used to make in any way I could. The strange thing was, when we moved in, we used to sleep in the same bed. It was a double we had been given by my brother and it was a nice bed, but when we would go to bed, I would get close and put my arm round her and she would say, "Move back on your own side; you're making me hot", so I didn't think much of it. We had sex like other people - she was 'one position only', on her back and you could give her oral sex but she wouldn't give you oral sex. It was crazy. I carried on because we had a baby, but I was fighting a losing battle, so, we got the house for £8000 and got the mortgage for £12000 and we had lived in it for 2 months when a lady came and offered me £50,000 cash. I said no because it had taken me two years to do and I wanted to live in it. Her dad said, "You're mad! You could have got one near me for £50k," but I said no because I had put in two years hard work and wanted to enjoy what I had done. Then my wife said, "I don't know why we don't sell", and I said, "Because it wasn't you working on this house until midnight every day you could, that's why." So, I was trying to do my work and play rugby and my wife was with her mum 7 days a week so even if I came home, there was no one there. It was strange looking back - my mum never made me sandwiches for work and after getting married, I thought that maybe my wife would, but no. She used to say, "If you want them, make them yourself". I said, "Fuck me, it's two rounds of bread with a bit of ham on. You don't have to make a fire and slow-turn a pig for 12 hours! Just put a slice of ham in between two slices of bread - you don't even need to butter it!" and she said, "Well, if it's that easy, make them yourself". So, I could see what type of marriage this was going to be, but to be truthful, I worked 7 days a week and trained 5 nights, played Saturday after work or Sunday after work and went for a drink so I didn't see much of her which was a good thing because there was always something wrong or she wanted something.

Working with my family, a 7-day week was compulsory and if you asked, "Can I have Saturday or Sunday off?" he would say, "If you don't want to do it, go home and don't come back." It was fine by me because I had done it all my life. I didn't know anything else and I loved my job and we got on well and had a good laugh and the money wasn't great but you did jobs after work to earn extra money. It was hard but that was life; I just got on with it. I used to go into the wholesalers and get a coffee and load my big coat up with tools; good tools, mind, I never took any shit. Don't get me wrong, if they saw me, I would go to the counter and he would tell me to put it back. I did it a lot with stuff he would see, like a six-foot level, and have it down my pants and up the side of my coat going past my ear. Then he would laugh like fuck and tell me to put the fucker back so really, I was toying with them so I would know if I was clear or not. He even caught me carrying an oven downstairs in the back and I was going to put it in my van and he said, "What are you doing with that?" I said, "I am bringing it into the shop to ask you how much it was", and he wouldn't believe me, so I dropped it on the ground and told him I would just get one at B&Q. He said sorry to me, but I got in the van and drove off.

I needed 30 x 8-foot lengths of 3x2 timber for a job at the weekend, so I drove in, put them all nice and neat on the van and covered then over with a 5mm sheet of plyboard. I pulled up outside and said to him, "Do you want to check how thick that ply is?" He said, "No, I can see it's 5mm by the way it bends." I stood talking to him about the game I had played in on Saturday and when I was leaving, I shouted, "Don't forget to book that ply, mate," and he said okay, so, I drove home, dropped the wood off and then drove back with the ply, parked outside the office, knocked on the window and lifted it off the back of the pick-up. Then I took it into the timber shed and put it back. I went back in and he asked what was up and I said the joiner had picked one up from the other place, so we don't need it. We were still doing the same thing; working, then going to another job after 5 pm and working till 9 pm then the pub, 2 pints and home. But didn't get paid overtime and when I asked, he said, "I took you for a pint." I said, "I didn't want one. I can't take a pint to the bank and say 'take that off my mortgage'," so he said, "Find yourself another job, then". So, it carried on and after a couple of years, we ended up moving to a new house. We had some money saved up and the jobs I was doing after work were adding up to the money pot, so we looked at one that was £52,000 and when we put ours up, we got £44,000. I know I could have sold for £50,000 two years before, but I could not go through it again, working till all hours, so we did the deal; £44,000 for mine and we paid £50,000 for the new one. Problem one: we went to view it one night when it was dark and it looked half good and my wife never shut up about how close it was to her mum so I had to buy it. Then came moving day and my mate helped me but when we moved in, oh my God, it was a fucking shambles! A timber kitchen extension with a tin roof and every carpet in the house was filthy. The wife starts, "What the fuck's up with you now?" and I said, "It's a shit hole!" She said, "You knew it needed some jobs doing". Then, when I said it would be better to pull it down, she just walked out and went to her mum's with the 2-year-old baby. So, then I would work until 11 pm – midnight, have a wash, drop a mattress on the floor then get up at 5 am, have a couple of hours to do some bits, then bagging all the shit, then I was off to work with my pick-up full of bags of shit from my house around 7.40 am so I could put my shit in the skip in the works yard before anyone came in. I asked the wife to help me paint the skirting boards but she said, "I am not getting full of paint!" It was a fucking joke! Mind you, she didn't mind showing people round when I had got the first part done, so long as she was all done up with her make up on and nails painted.

Once me and our kid had found some things to make us money, I did do the place up again. I would save up then give her the £1000 and tell her to get better carpets then next, get a better three-piece, but she never looked happy. I was still going out with the lads and training in the week and taking her out on a Saturday but most of the time, she would come home with a face on her for something stupid. It was very rare she came home and wanted to sleep together. We were still having sex but after sex, she would go into the other room and sleep with my daughter in a double bed. I thought it was the thing people did and it was to keep my daughter asleep but it wasn't. The sex was shite anyway; some of the times we had sex, she would watch tv over my shoulder but I thought it was normal and she used to say to me, "That's all you want to do," and it was. One night, she said it wouldn't bother her if she never had sex again and I thought what a strange person she was. I wanted sex every day and I wanted to do what everyone was doing in the videos but there was no chance at that. Her exact words were, "I AM NOT A PORN STAR".

After a few years of marriage, we had another child and later on, I even extended the box room over the porch so I could sleep in there. Then, after a couple of years, she put my second daughter in that room. I doubled up on the garage and turned that into my bedroom. How bad does that sound? Married and both in separate rooms after two years! Even her mum said to her that it was not healthy for a marriage, but she said, "I don't care; he snores". It was okay shoving money in her hand and it was okay to go and stay in a fancy hotel. She would sleep in the same bed then. At this time, I was going through a difficult time at work as I was getting paid the same as other people for doing a lot more, so I left.

My wife had not long had our second child, but things were different from the first time. She just didn't treat her like she had the first one. She was very strict and offhand with her and just left her to cry. That made me feel bad because I was at work 7 days a week, but I was providing a good life for them and that is what I wanted to do; make sure my kids had what I never had, no matter what it was or what it cost. As they both got older, she treated the second girl worse and that was the only time we would row if I came in and she had been treating her like shit. My youngest was scared of the dark but the wife wasn't bothered about walking into her bedroom and switching her lamp off, and if she cried in the night, it was me that she wanted. This brought back so many memories of when I was a child and looking for love, it was crazy. I used to try my best to get home before she went to bed so she knew I was in the house and I would go upstairs and sit on the floor at the side of her bed, and she would go to sleep with her hand on my head. Thinking about this now kills me; poor little thing was bullied to an inch of her life and by someone who was spoiled all her life.

The thing was, she was adorable. Everyone loved the little one; she was so friendly and cute and very kind-hearted. My oldest was tough and more like a tomboy so she could look after herself but my youngest was an easy target for anyone to bully and that is what my wife was doing. She would say things to her like, "Your Daddy will be home soon so you can cry to him." These were just things you wouldn't put a child through. No wonder the poor girl had no confidence; she had knocked it out of her. She was a brilliant dancer but wanted to change dances. Her mum said no, she could carry on with the one she was doing. When I asked her why, she said the dress had cost £400. So, I said, "The dress I bought in the first place can be taken back and she can change dance!" Then she said, "Oh, Daddy's little girl is not happy," so I reminded her that it was our job to make sure both our kids were happy – it wasn't all about her!

We ended up selling the dress and I bought her the stuff she needed to change dance and said to the wife, "Keep the money off the dress and get yourself something that may cheer you up", then I went back to work.

I went working for Pilks for 6 years and on afternoons, I would climb out of the window and get into my van, go to my brother-in-law, give him my clock card as he was on days and get him to clock me on at 10 am next day. Then I would go in for 1 pm and get my card off him and tell the boss my card did not clock me off last night so I would gain 3 free hours. Or, if he came on after my night turn, we finished at 5.40 am, I would ask him to clock me off at 7.40 am and pick my card up later. I had some good times there. I used to take my van on site on night shift and load it with scrap and blue tissue rolls. These I used to take to my barber and he used to shave my hair for free. I did take the ink and solvent from there to the clothes printers and he would print T-shirts free for me and I would go into the works stores and get boxes of T-shirts and sell them to the factory. They did use liquid silver but this was hard to get hold of and when I did find out where it was, one of my close mates was already taking it so I did not go on his patch.

So, in the end, I got a job as a chargehand over a new part of the plant. One night, we were having problems and I had to go over to the other side of the machine. On my way back over the stairs, I slipped down some stairs and hurt my wrist and neck, but I was also getting bad headaches and I had started to shake so they tested me for Parkinson's again and that put an end to my job too. This was now the first time I had been out of work.

The shaking was getting worse and worse, even when I tried to drink anything and I went to the doctors. He sent me for a scan but I couldn't wait so I had to go private. They found out a disc had come out of my neck completely and was resting on my spinal cord and nerves, so he said to me, "If you don't have it taken out, the next time you fall over you will cut through your spinal cord and you will be paralysed from the neck down. It is your choice." So, I had to have the disc removed. They went through the side of my throat to do it and I had 15 staples. The day I had it done, I felt great. It was the day after when I was hit by pain you can't describe and when I tried to sleep, I dozed off, woke up and couldn't move anything from my neck down. I just lay crying. I couldn't get my buzzer for the nurse so had to wait until one came in. As soon as the door opened, I shouted him and he said, "Right, chill out, don't worry; the extra anaesthetic has worn off so this will hurt." He put his hand under my head and back and lifted me up. I screamed, so he said, "I will go and get you some relief now." He came back with the magic morphine and that helped for some time but I wouldn't go to sleep; after that, I sat up for the 4 days I was in there.

When I got home, I couldn't tip my head to drink water or anything so I had to smash my tablets up in a cup; morphine, codeine, diazepam, amitriptyline, gabapentin, naproxen and a few others. They were mashed up in a cup with hot water and I used to sit on the edge of the bed and wait for them to kick in - around 8 minutes - then fix all the pillows so I could sit up in bed and watch tv. That was my life - for 6 months, I was fucked. I had gone from training 6 days a week and playing rugby, to sitting in a bed like a crack addict. It was not nice. Then bang! The depression kicked in; just sat on your own in bed. It was awful - all I wanted to do was die. I had lost everything and I had nothing left to live for; that's all I used to think. My wife didn't give a fuck. She just left me alone every day and even when I told her I wanted to die, she said, "Don't talk stupid", but I had nothing left. I had lost my job, all my work on the side, my bits of income and I'd ended up on sick pay.

I was in bed for 6 months. I was a mess. I had to drink everything through a straw and still my ever-loving wife went out every day and left me alone in bed in agony. My other little girl was now 4 but the wife said, "I won't make same mistake this time," and just let her cry, told her off and treated her like shit and I saw this as I was at home a lot. Anytime I would say something, she would say, "Go on, little princess, to your daddy." It was strange; we never argued but I used to end up in one when she treated the youngest like shit. Poor girl didn't know what to do for the best. Most nights, she would send her to bed and when I went up, she would be crying and it was breaking my heart. I had a huge row with my wife and I said, "You have no fucking idea what you're putting that poor girl through. You talk to her nicely then you talk to her like shit; she doesn't know what fucking day it is with you. Just leave her alone." All this was going on because my wife was a spoiled little bitch all her life and spoke to her own parents like shit so she couldn't get out of the habit. She couldn't stop treating my youngest like shit. My oldest girl was not bothered; she just gave the shit back to her but my youngest was scared of her. She was totally out of order, so I used to take my youngest out in the van to price jobs to get her away from the wife and that brought back memories of my own mum and my sisters taking me out to get me away from her. I couldn't believe this was happening! If I had had the money, I would have moved away with my youngest to get away from her because she was a control freak.

My full life had gone - I had lost everything; my friends, my job, my rugby career, my social life and my health. I was in a bad place and it is very hard to get out of it. I had no support from my wife; she would sleep in the other room, get up, make me a drink of tea and leave a flask of hot water for me to take my tablets first thing and later on. Then at 10.30 am, the front door shut and she would go out with her mum all day. I had thought many times about ending it, I was in so much pain and I couldn't control the pain. I used to sit on the bed and cry because I didn't deserve this. I hadn't hurt anyone - I always looked after people, so, at one of my low points, I got 1000mg of morphine ready in warm water and wrote a note to say, 'I am sorry but I can't cope anymore' and went into the back garden and sat on the wall trying to pluck up courage to suck up the morphine through the straw. Something fell on the floor in the kitchen and it was loud because the floor was laminate, so I got up and went into the kitchen. On the floor was a bottle with a pink folded note inside, only 40mm wide. It was from my youngest daughter to me for Valentine's Day. I took the top off and it had a little note inside so I sat outside reading it and it made me upset and got me to think about my two kids and how it would kill them. Also, I couldn't leave my youngest because she was too timid and was bullied most days by her mum. I think she got a kick out of making her cry. Even if she was sick, she would drag her to school. It was only when she would be sick all over the school that she was allowed home. the poor girl went through hell and I understood how she felt because I had gone through the same thing.

So, I went outside and tipped the morphine drink down the drain and decided to start getting out; first by just going for a walk with the kids, then going through the day just to get some fitness back. It took me a long time to get back on track and start to do some building work a bit at a time, then to get my own company running again, but I was still getting treatment for depression. I had to handle it my way, so I slowly started to work more and more days and then started going to the gym, made new friends and slowly started to build my company back up and make a good name for myself.

After getting over my operation, I started doing building work and I got more and more and ended up with a kitchen fitter doing his plumbing and electrics. His pay was good but he was just strange. Anyway, I wanted a new kitchen myself and got some prices and the guy who I had been working with was spot on, so he said, "How are you going to work it?" and I said, "Give me a couple of weeks". So, I said to the wife, "Listen, we cannot afford this kitchen, so I am going to have to do it another way. How do you fancy moving in with your mum for the 6 weeks school holidays?" She asked me why but I promised to tell her later.

My plan was to put the chip pan on and let it damage the wall while I was sat at the computer, so I went out of the French doors, looked inside the kitchen window and fuck me, the full kitchen had gone up, so I got the hose pipe and tried to get in the window with the hose. Then, as I pulled the trigger, the flames were getting bigger and bigger, but I was stuck in the PVC window and by the time I had got out, the firemen had kicked the door down and I was on the floor in the back garden, so they put me on oxygen and our kid came round. He was a superstar, so they all hung round him having photos taken with my famous relation! In the end, I had to rip out all downstairs and the hall, stairs and landing, so I redid the front room and fitted a new kitchen, new ceilings and tiles, new everything! I also knocked through to the garage under the stairs and fitted a shower room. I wanted fitted oak flooring through the living room and hall, so for this, I went into B&Q, loaded 18 packs on my trolley along with all the underlay and 12 oak beads, then walked through the till and paid around £1400 on my credit card. I then took it to the van, loaded it all in and walked back into the store. I then loaded 18 packs, the underlay and beads onto my trolley and when she was busy on returns, I joined the queue. When I got to the counter, she said, "You only got these 25 minutes ago!" I asked how she knew that and she said, "It's on the receipt," so I explained and said, "I took it outside and the wife said it looked too dark for her and we have just had a huge fall out and I told her to go and get her own stuff!" So, the woman scanned my receipt. I even offered to help her put the items back but she said it was okay. Again, the house was empty while I was doing the front room with no help. It took me 10 hours, but it looked awesome! When she came home, I was bagging the offcuts and she said, "Have you not finished yet?" and I said, "I am cleaning up", so she said, "I will get a shower then while you clean up." It was soul-destroying; zero fucking help at all; she was one lazy bitch.

I was starting to do jobs for people who could not afford the work so I would get all their insurance documents, take them home, study them and go back and tell them what to do. The first couple had a leak from the shower and the ceiling was stained so I said, "You will need a little bit more water down". She didn't understand, so I said, "Right, you go out shopping and when you come back, ring the insurance." So, while she was out, I disconnected the feed going to the toilet so it was coming through the windows through to walls. My mate said, "That's got to be it," and I said, "Just sit in the van, pal. I will sort it." So, after around 20 minutes, it was a disaster, so I shut the door and got in the van and drove off. Next thing, this woman rang and was crying on the phone. She just kept saying, "What have you done to my house?" So, we ended up going back and I dealt with the insurance as though I was her husband, but we took all the carpets out of the living room, hall and stairs and laminate in the kitchen and took out the full kitchen so she had a brand-new house within 8 days - new kitchen, re-wired, re-decorate all the way through, new carpets and new kitchen flooring, and at the end, I said to her, "What are your thoughts now?" and she said, "It is stunning, thank you." This made me very good money - I had purchased the kitchen from B&Q, so I went into the store on the Bank Holiday Monday as I thought it would be packed. I put all the units and the doors with the taps and sink on the trolley and took them back to returns. I had to wait as there was a queue, but I needed the main door to open so it looked like I had just walked in, so I joined the que and when I got to the front, the lady asked if there was anything wrong with the stuff and I said, "No, love, she is over there. Now, she doesn't like the doors and wants to move the units round so one of your kitchen people is looking at her drawing and they are going to change it round so I will be back through in a minute. Can you just give me a credit note as I have to buy another one?" She said, "Sorry, love, but I have to refund you on your card, and you will have to just put the other one through", so she went through everything and refunded £1720 onto my card. I said thank you then I walked into the store, mobile phone at my ear, saying, "I am just coming to you now. Are you still with the kitchen man?" and I walked off. I then walked round the store and out of the exit door. I was well made up with myself.

It was nearly springtime and the wife said we needed some garden furniture, so I said took her to my favourite shop and got a large round teak table with 4 teak adjustable chairs, 2 teak loungers, a cast base for the brolly and a new large brolly. Then we picked up all the cushions for all the furniture and the wife said, "This will cost, you know", and I said it was okay so we went through and it cost me just over £2000. We put everything in the van, took it home and put it all up, then I drove to the tip, got rid of all the boxes and went back to the shop. I put everything we had just purchased onto a large trolley and went back to returns. When it came to me, the woman asked if there was anything wrong with it and I said, "You know what, love? My wife has just bought this and we live in a terraced house. If I put the table in the garden, the chairs won't fit round it. Women have no idea of what space is." She started to laugh and said, "It is lovely furniture though," and I said, "It is if you have the house or space to put it in!" She scanned it all and put it back on my card.

Before I forget, we had had it two years and the recliners had broken so I took them back and said to the woman, "How long a warranty do I get with this furniture? I have not had it 12 months," and she said, "I will have to get the manager"! I wondered if I should just leave it and walk off but it was too late, he being at my side, so I had to bang on about each chair costing me nearly £300 and he apologised and said, "We don't do this anymore", so I said, "Great! Left with stuff to burn!" Then he said, "While you don't have your receipt, I will give you £550 in vouchers and you can buy the chairs back for the other £50 then you can try to get them fixed." So, I came home with the 2 recliners I took plus £550 in vouchers; what a result!

I then started to do insurance fire and floods for everyone. It got out of hand as I was doing one a month and clearing £15000 to £20000. We started to pick the units up from a kitchen company and load them in from the back of the van. One lad would stand at the back loading and, because the van was backed into the warehouse, you could open the side sliding door and drag in fridge freezers and cookers off the pile at the side. You just had to wait until the stack in the van was high enough, so, after a bit, we just hung a black curtain across the front quarter of the van so you couldn't see what I was doing at the side. By doing this, we were making around £1200 for the fit, then the electrics, the plumbing and the tiling, so if you got the fridge freezer and cooker, that was close to another £1100. That way, we could come off a job earning £1500 cash for 7 days' work.

I remember doing one job that was to be a fire. I told him to make sure he had a chip pan and get 3 blocks of lard as it has a lower temp combustion rate than oil. So, what does he do? Gets the pan and 3 large bottles of oil! He rang me and said, "Mate, I am struggling. The house is full of white smoke", and I said, "You have bought oil then?" and he said, "Yes, I didn't think it would make any difference". I told him to open the back gate and open the back door. I drove a couple of miles out of the town and walked in. You couldn't breathe! He was panicking like hell, but I was just laughing. I said, "Come outside because when I throw this in, it will go with a bang due to the heat and the smoke", so, I lit a cloth, popped open the door and threw it in and said to him, "Give it 3 minutes then ring the firemen". Then I drove back to my job. I rang him after a bit and he said they were inside, so I said, "Just keep out of the way. You were making tea and fell asleep on the sofa. I will see you tomorrow." The next day, it had ripped the place apart. The kitchen had nothing left, the ceiling and bathroom floor had gone and the bath had melted and was on the kitchen floor, so we got all the prices done, won the job and he got a completely new house; full re-wire, new water main, new central heating and all the walls plastered and brand-new stairs. We got it all painted and I said, "It is down to you now, mate, to use your contents money to get your carpets and all your bits and bobs of stuff." Another happy customer! I was doing this for a couple of years and the money I was saving was getting very high - over £200k - but I wanted to hit one million before I was 50 years old; that was my goal. All the time I was doing this, I was looking after family, giving them money. If I went out with the lads, I would take £400 and spend it on us lot. The wife had the best of everything and so did the kids. She didn't like what I was doing but didn't mind spending the money; but aren't all women like that? We still subcontracted to my cousins' company and they were doing big council jobs and some warehouse work. We were sent to a warehouse that supplied all the small shops. It led all sorts of stuff, so I told my mate to empty the big toolbox and bring it in as it was on two wheels. Because we were fitting lights, we got in the scissor lift and went to the top. Every aisle had a camera looking down it, but we were higher than the camera and higher than the fence at the side that kept all the cigarettes inside so I leaned over, got a box, opened it and filled the toolbox and the empty light fitting box and left the old light on the scissor lift. After we had done a couple in that row, I told him just to put the stuff in the empty light fitting boxes, that way, we could empty the chocolate boxes into them then put the empty ones back on the shelf so no one would notice.

After, we got a big renovation job at the hospital farm and it had huge building on there that they used for different things for the hospital. We had to lay new floors and a damp course but it was built out of sandstone so it was hard work. I was on with my older brother whom I used to make good money with, so we got stuck in and had a look round. In one of the barns, there was a huge generator on the back of a trailer, same as the ones at the fairground, so, we asked about it and it was the back-up for the hospital emergency lighting. It was worth £36,000 but all the wheels on the trailer were flat so we talked to a couple of people we knew and one guy said, "I will give you £10,000 for it", so we went back one weekend after work, pumped all the tyres up and put it on the tow bar on the big van. The problem was the weight - the van was struggling to pull it and we had to travel 4 miles with it so he got at the back of me with his hazard lights on and I towed it to this man's yard, parked it up and moved our van away. He came out and started it and it ran! The engine was spotless; all painted green. All of a sudden, he said, "I don't want it", and I thought our kid was going to knock him out! He came up with all sorts of reasons so we ended up getting £2000 for it and we left then went for a drink. My brother was going mad but I told him to leave it. However, the week after, we found out he had taken the engine off the trailer and connected it to his yard to run all his electric!

Even more, though, he sold the trailer for £4000! He was a big, fat, greedy arsehole but he ended up killing himself operating a large digger, so he got a lesson of his own.

The next place we ended up was at a chemical site in Liverpool. They supplied everything you could think of and because of all the jobs I could do, the owner loved me. If they were really busy, I would even have my lads packing chemicals for his site and delivering the orders. I got on great with his accountant and he said, "Just knock me an invoice up for whatever your cost is each week and I will pay you cash just to get rid of it," so I made the invoice up on my computer - after all, he didn't care what company it was from - and he gave me £1750 for the week's work with 4 others lads. I told him to keep the £50 and get a nice bottle of wine for him and the wife and you would have thought I had given him £500! The chemicals they sold were things like bleach, washing-up liquid and rat poison, so I got rid of a lot to people I knew. I met a bloke who converted motorhomes so I got him these large plastic containers to strap to the bottom of the motorhome for fresh water and I used to give all the garages surgical gloves and cleaner for their floors then I would get my van fixed and punctures repaired free but that's how I liked to work.

Now, this company couldn't get enough of me no matter what it was they asked me to do, from building a new 20-metre storeroom to fitting a tap in the toilets. In fact, they were hitting me with so much work I was struggling to cope so I had to bring in more and more men. I was paying them £30 a day and charging £90 a day for labour and £200 a day for tradesmen. So, I took their accountant a case of wine and said, "Can you help me out? I am going to struggle to put all these men on the invoice for my company." He said, "You don't have to give me your invoice. I don't care what company is on it as long as it adds up to your total." So, that night, I sat at my computer for 3 hours and made up an invoice. I had 5 tradesmen in and 4 labourers and some had only worked Saturday and two of us had worked Sunday, but I put everyone in for 7 days and charged £9480 including VAT. When I took it to him, he paid the invoice and I gave him back some cash to take his wife out for a night. He was shocked because it was over £500. He said, "We will sit down next week and go through some stuff. I will look after you now." I told him, "It's a two-way street, but I will be grateful of your help, mate.

Have a good weekend". When I got home and went through the costings, I think my wage bill for the week was £1700 so I made a lot of money.

I had a good mate working with me, Big Paul; he was a class joiner and I was teaching him electrics but he hated going near electrics. I had re-wired the new office and I was showing Paul but he wouldn't go near the fuse board because they were the big old 1920's fuses, so I used to do the boards. Then, they asked me to fit a new battery charger for the fork truck but it was 3 face. Paul said, "Mate, I will help you fit the big cable but I am not going near the board". So, we fitted a big 4-core cable about 20 metres away from the charger. I wired the switch on the charger and climbed up on the scaffold to get to the board Paul asked me, "Why is it called 4 core?" so I said, "Come up the scaffold and I will show you". When he got up, I explained which were the live wires and which was the earth. I told him about the earth bars to isolate the wires, then I said, "These three bars are all separate lives," and I touched one with the screwdriver. Then I turned to him and said, "Keep away from the neutral and the earth," and I moved the driver to the right and the earth was loose. The flash lit the room up, blew my screwdriver apart and threw me to the back of the scaffolding on my arse. I looked up and Paul was getting down. I said, "What are you doing?" and he said, "Mate, I am not interested in electrics. I would sooner stay alive!" I got up and went to get another driver and finished the job. I asked Paul to turn it on and he refused so I had to turn it on. It started buzzing and that was it He said, "I can't believe you went back and finished that! I would have just gone home and said I felt sick."

We did have some good times in there. No one questioned anything, so you could arrive at 8 am, tell the boss you were on site, go off and plaster a living room, change your clothes and get back about 4.15 pm, just in time to knock off!

They had loads of vans and big trucks and I took three fuel cards out of each van; then I got a plate made up for each and I used to hang it on my own reg plate before going to the petrol station. The girls in the station knew what I was doing so I used to put fuel in their cars and they were made up, so, no matter what I took, even if it had petrol in, they would book diesel for me. In the end, I got 9 years out of those cards. Then one day, one of the lads who works there phoned and asked if I had one of their fuel cards. He said that the new owner was going to get the police involved as the girl in the petrol station had identified me as using their card. So, I said, "Meet me in town near the bank." We had a coffee and I said, "Right, you need to help me here, mate. Here is £200 and here is 2 grams of cocaine; now, go back and tell them that the agreement with your old company was I uses my van for your deliveries, and you gave me a fuel card." After he left, I thought, 'Shit, I hope this works or I am fucked if they send the police' as I had 60 x 25ltr drums of diesel in my brother's garage! Anyway, around 4 pm he rings and said, "I have no idea where you pulled that from, but I walked into his office and said, 'Here is that card back. We used to use the builders for years and they used their van dropping our stuff off.' I told him the builders didn't mind as long as we paid their fuel."

The next week, just to repay him for saving me from the police or prosecution, I gave him £500 and a £100 bag of coke and he was made up. After all, I had not paid for any fuel for around 9 years so that was a huge saving.

Back then, I was very well known due to my rugby and my building company and I got asked a couple of times if I would start selling cocaine due to the amount of people who knew me. I said no at the time, but looking back, I think I would have made more money doing that than doing the building work because everybody knew me throughout the town; that's why my name can't go in this book.

When the wife and I went out on a Saturday night, there would be about 6 to 10 couples and I always took out around £400 and after we had all had a few drinks, I use to buy everyone drinks, even people who was stood at the bar. I didn't care but my wife used to go mad about me throwing money away, but she was okay when I gave her £1000 to go shopping with her mum, even though she still never bought anything for me. She was a spoiled, greedy, controlling, bullying bitch and I have no idea why the fuck I was with her. I was a joker when I was out and get everyone laughing. I even used to strip off and walk round the pub; I didn't care. We had a good laugh, but she would just sit there with a bad look on her face and when it came time to going home, she would moan all the way home, complaining about my behaviour on that night and I think that was just her saying you're not having sex again. That seemed to be her way of bargaining and it was a constant problem. Once we were home, she would take off her make up and get undressed then come back downstairs with a dressing gown on, make a cup of coffee and go back to bed on her own and I would sit there with my shirt and tie watching TV at 2 o'clock in the morning. I was always up for 7 am to get my stuff loaded onto the van and into work for 7.45 am; no cup of tea or toast, just back to work and when I would get home, she would be at her mum's for dinner so I would go to the pub and meet the lads on Sunday afternoon about 1 pm, then back home to bed, up at 6 pm and out with the lads at 7.30 pm after my youngest had gone to bed. On Sunday night, we would have a scream. There could be anything from 12 to 30 of us but we had a great time. All we did was laugh and take the piss out of each other but it set you up for the week coming.

My good mate had just got a new job at The Big Food Company. They used to do deliveries to all the big supermarkets, so they had loads of items from steak to tampons. We were out one weekend and he said, "I am off tomorrow, then I have two 12-hour days and then two 12-hour nights then four days off". I said, "Fuck me, 4 days off? That's great!" said he asked, "Do you fancy doing something one night?" and I said, "Yes, no problem". Then he said, "I will ring you on Thursday morning around 3 am, so if it's on, you get up, if not, stay asleep." When the call came through, I had to go and meet the wagon driver on the industrial estate just off the East Lancs Road. When I got there, a security man came out and said, "You come to meet the driver?" and I said, "Yes, mate", so I drove in and when I got to the trailer, he had already unloaded 4 cages of products. Two were full of wine and champagne, then there was a mixture of deodorant and every food, even down to chewing gum, so I loaded my van, drove home and backed to my garage. I was wiped out, so I went to bed, had a couple of hours then went out when my mate came and unloaded the full van into the garage. I had already taken 10 boxes of white wine through to my shed and plenty of deodorant for me, the wife and girls and took some of the chocolate and put it in the cupboard. Later on, he called round and told me to help myself to whatever I wanted, but I said I would rather he was there too, so he gave me another 10 cases of wine and asked if I wanted champagne. I said, No, mate, no one likes it," but I had already taken two boxes. He told me a bloke would be round tomorrow to clear everything out. The next day, when I came home, the wife told me he had left some money for me in the drawer and when I looked, he had left me £600 so I rang him and said, "Mate, you don't have to give me this - the wine and the other stuff was enough," and he said, "No, mate, you're getting a cut too as you're the driver. There is another one Tuesday morning, same time, same place but wait till I ring you." I was meeting him for a pint later and he told me not to mention it while we were out, so we met the lads later and just had a good laugh all night. The next one was just 4 cages of wine and a cage of meat and when we loaded my van, it was on its arse with all the boxes of wine plus the cage of meat but I still had to drive it home and park at the front of my garage. Then he rang me and said, "Mate, unload as soon as you can and get back". Again, it was 4 cages of wine and spirits and a cage of mixed items, so, we got it loaded and I said, "This won't fit in my garage, pal. I will leave it in my van and use my mate's van tomorrow." I pulled up and stripped what I could off the mixed cage and took another 10 cases of wine, a case of brandy and a case of vodka and put them in my shed. The next day, he rang and said, "I need your van, mate, if it's full." I told him I had left the key on top of the back wheel, so he got the van and dropped it off somewhere, then, as I got home, he was loading the van again and I started helping him. Once he was finished, he told me to keep what was left, so I moved the items into my house out of the way. Then he came back to mine and said, "Here, pal, take your keys and this is yours", and he gave me £2500! I told him to take some back as I was just the driver, but he said, "We couldn't do it without you, and I don't trust anyone else. Besides, I am making a lot more money than you are!" So I said, "As long as you are getting the bigger share, that's all I want." We did this twice or three times a month for over a year and I was giving everybody I knew wine, but the wife told me to stop giving it away because her and her mum liked it, so we were fully loaded with all the drinks, loads of ladies' deodorant, razors and electric toothbrushes. We even had 24 cases of shower gel! It was great - we wanted for nothing.

The wife was asking for new flooring at home because everyone was getting laminate, so I went to B&Q and did my usual routine. I bought the laminate and everything else I needed, then the next day, I loaded up the trolley with the same stuff and went to the returns desk. The assistant asked if there was anything wrong and I said, "No, she just bought the wrong one. I wanted beech to match the doors." She refunded the price onto my card, then I left, heading to pick up the other colour, waited till I was out of sight then nipped out the exit and home – another room done for nothing! After I had done this room, I wanted some for the bedroom I had built over the garage for me to sleep in, so I just went back and went through the same procedure and got the floor for the bedroom. This one only cost a little over £700 but again, it was a good saving for me. When she came home, she didn't help me to clean up or anything. I had to put the furniture back myself and all she could say was that the gas fire needed changing, and I said, "No, it needs cleaning," and she said, "Well, clean it then", so I just walked off and got a shower and went upstairs to watch tv. Next day, I went to B&Q and looked at the gas fires. I thought I would get the one that cost more so I put it on my trolley, paid for it, then went home and fitted it. I then took the empty box back to the store. This time, I went through the trade entrance and asked, "Do I bring this back here?" and said the lady said, "No, love, you have to go down to the entrance and to returns." She rang and told the woman, "I have a man coming down with a gas fire," and she told her the model, so I walked into the store, back down the gas fire aisle and swapped the empty box for a full one. Then I took it back to returns and the lady said, "Is it all okay?" and I said, "I didn't open it, love; it's the wrong fire - we need a flueless one," so she refunded it back onto my card. I went back to my own work and put all my bags of shite into their skip. When I got home after going to the gym, she didn't even notice that I had fitted a new fire, so I just said nothing and went to bed.

I started to go training on a night with my mates; it wasn't to get big; it was just a break from work and home. We all used to meet around 5.20 pm and do around 45 minutes and then into the sauna and jacuzzi but the changing room was huge and by the time we were going home, there weren't many people in, so we used to tip the cold drink machine forward to get us all a drink. One Friday night, I was there on my own and thought I would have a go on the stand-up sunbed so I put all my stuff in my locker and went inside. On the wall was the coin box and I looked at it and thought, 'I am sure I can get into this', so I went back out and got my bag, and, in the side pocket were some home-made keys I had been using for a few years. I put my stuff away and went back into the sunbed. There were only two blokes getting changed in the changing room but it was a little noisy using the keys, so I put a pound coin in the box to get the sunbed going and I turned on the radio that was inside it. Then, going back to the box, I changed keys for a smaller one and it opened first time. When you took the box out, it told you on the screen how much money was in the box and it came up £342, so I put all the coins into my towel and put £8 back in and locked the box. I then had 3 minutes on the bed, so I went home after and put all the coins in the middle drawer in my office and left £10 worth in my gym bag and left it at that. I was out Saturday night with the wife, and I was working Sunday so after work, I headed for the gym and had a shower, a sauna and then nipped to the sunbed. When I opened the coin box, it was full again, so I took out around £300 and left the rest in and went home for dinner. In the week, I was telling one of my mates that I could get into that box and get us free sunbeds, so I would go in first and open it. Early in the week there was not much in it so I would take out £8 and put £2 in for me and go out and give each one £2. I would always take my bag in with me now and on Friday, around 6.30 pm to 7 pm when it was quiet, the box always had over £320 in and I was taking £300 out and going back on Sunday because it was full again after the weekend. By then, I had worked out how to zero the numbers on the coin box. After doing this for a long time, one night, we walked into the changing rooms and there were two blokes stood inside the sunbed booth, with the manager outside, saying, "We have not got a clue what's going on as it is giving us all sorts of readings and there is nothing in the box but I know people do use it". One of the blokes with suits on said, "The box may be faulty; we will change the box". We all went into the sauna and we were laughing like kids and the lads were saying how they knew they would catch on. Funny thing was, we were the only four people in the gym who were tanned well in April! After the box was changed, you had to buy a token from reception so that was another scam stopped. I tried to get rid of all the pound coins but there were so many that even the bank would not take them. I had to put them into the company account just to get rid of them.

I did have a bit of a fall out with the manager; I didn't like him. I asked him a question in the showers one night and he told me he had finished working for the day and wouldn't answer. That pissed me off big time. Anyway, they had just set up a big stand outside the changing room with all the new running shoes on display, but only the left foot, so each night, I took one off and put it in my bag until I had cleaned the display out of 18 brand-new left foot shoes. I was hoping they would put out the other foot so I could take them, but they didn't; they just took the stand down! I even went upstairs to the shop to see if there were any right foot shoes on display as I could have put them in my bag, but they only had left ones so I took the lot to work and threw them in the big compactor never to be seen again. That is what happens when you piss me off.

One night we were working out near the dumbbells and he came over and said, "Can you put these back after you have used them?" and I said, "I would if I had used them but I didn't", and he walked off. I was so pissed off that I went for a shower before heading for the sauna. I ripped half the pipes out of the wall so there was water going everywhere. When I got into the sauna, my mate came in gave me a drink and said, "Have you been renovating the showers?" and I said, "How did you know?" and he said, "As soon as I walked in and the changing room was flooded, I knew someone had pissed Tuck off big time." I would have loved to knock the manager out, but we just had a laugh about it.

Through working for a few companies, I had picked things up very quick so I could now do plumbing and I was great with electrics. I would go and do loads of electrical jobs as they paid good money, but I was more interested in how people used to fiddle the electricity companies.

We worked on a couple of homes where they had two electric meters - one for the electric man to read, and one in his garage running all the big items in his house. I worked with the same spark for two years and we had loads of talks about it. You could sometimes find an electricity man who would fit two cables for you as long as you had the meter so he could go straight to it. He would fit you one for £350 but you had to get everything back-filled as soon as he had finished, even down to getting the flags laid. That made the installer happy as his work was covered up. So, I asked my mate, "Could we join into the incoming cable with our own?" and he said, "No, as it is permanent live so never goes off. You would have to get the right stuff; the gloves, the clamp and the right wellies, or it would blow out the bottom of your feet and it may kill you." So, I said, "What if we got into the cable higher up and put a 6mm hole in it, drilled through the wall and pushed back a 6mm cable and shoved it in the 6mm hole?" and he said, "You can do what you want as long as I am 20 feet away from you!" Then he laughed and said, "What the fuck goes on inside your head? Do you never switch off from scamming something?" and I replied, "No, mate, it's life and what I am used to doing." In the end, I managed to give the customer a 16-way board with only 8 fuses to cut down his bills but still give him the safety needed.

The customer wanted to introduce me to everyone and I said, "I can't, mate; it's dangerous, and if get caught because someone has told someone else, I am screwed. I only do things like this for people I really know well and have a good relationship with.", He said he understood, and a month later, he rang and said he wanted to meet me and my mate for a drink and a meal. When we met him, he had his mate with him so we went to the Indian, had some food then went back to another pub for a few drinks. He said to me, "I wish I could show you my electric bill from last month and this month; the difference is unreal!" I said that I was only in control of what came into his house. What he saved was up to him. Then he asked,

"How did you do it? We have looked all over it and can't find anything". I said, "That's why people ask me to do it. I know my work is good." said he said, "Good? Your work is the best I have ever seen, and I can get you loads of customers." I said, "I know that, but I vet each customer. I like to know where they work. how long they have been there, where did they work before and who they go out with. I know you're going to ask me to do your mate's, so I want to know the answer to all those questions and then some more after that." He said he understood then suggested I should charge more. I said, "I go off your bills and how long I have known you, and with yours, I know you and your wife; we have been out together a few times but all I know is your mate's name. I will get you a box you put on yourself and see what he is like with that for a few months." So, I took it his house, connected the earth and then fitted the live and his meter stopped and went backwards slowly. I said, "Right, everything you're using on the electric is free and this is sending the wheel back some; it will knock off around 3 to 4 days every 12 hours. Can you get me your last bill?" I looked at it and said, "When the wheel gets to this number, take off the live first then the earth because if you do it the other way round, you will end up in the kitchen." He said, "Fuck, mate, can you come back and do it for me?" So, I said, "Yes; ring me when you hit this number." About two weeks later, he rang and I disconnected it. I even told him what his next bill would be, and he said, "Can you sort it for me again?" I suggested he let it run for a month before we tried this again. He was made up and said, "My mate at work wants to meet you," but I said, "No, I don't do personal appearances. I will catch up with him down the line." He thanked me and off I went.

The best way to gain trust is to refuse something that you would normally take if you were offered.

For example, I was in the back of the canteen where they cook, and one of the ladies said, "Would you like a coffee, love?" and because I had seen big tins of coffee in the storeroom, I said, "Tea, please. I hate coffee." She gave me tea and said, "Would you like a chocolate bar with it?" and again I said, "No thanks, I hate chocolate." Again, I said this because the storeroom was full of it. There were about 6 people in the kitchen who had a brew with me so all these people now knew that I hate coffee and chocolate, so, after that, I finished my work but had to do some flooring to be done out of hours. All I needed for the flooring was my heat gun to weld the vinyl I had repaired, but I took in one big empty toolbox and two empty bags of floor screed blown up to look full as there was a camera facing the entrance. I cut the section out, fitted the new and welded the joint then cut the weld flat. Then I went into the walk-in fridge, filled my box with packs of bacon and pies and there was a padlock on the storeroom, so I unscrewed the hasp and staple, opened the door and then took 6 of everything out of every box and it was like going into a full sweetshop. I put two big tins of Nescafé in so both my empty bags were full. I came out, screwed back the hasp and staple and the doors were locked again. Then I put my stuff in the van, took it home and put the bacon in the freezer and all the sweets in the big drawer. I had to leave some in the bag. On the Monday, I went back into the canteen and said, "Is everything okay with the floor?" and the boss said, "Mate, you have done a cracking job. Do you want a brew?" I said, "Tea, please. I hate coffee." He gave me the tea and said, "Would you like a bar or something with that?" and one of the women said, "No, he doesn't like chocolate or sweets; that's why he has a body like that!" But then, I was in good shape.

We had to go into the builder's merchants because I had dropped my 4-foot level - if you drop them, they are no good, so I was standing at the tools and the lad behind the counter shouted, "I am fucking watching you,

Tucker!" and I said, "Okay, mate". I got a Stanley 4-foot level, slid it down my pants leg and tucked it into my rigger boots - that was £48. Then I put a plasterer's hammer down the other side - £28. Then I picked up a set of joiner's chisels and tried to walk but I couldn't because of the level, so I limped over and said, "Give me a coffee, mate, and how much are these for the set?" He passed me the coffee and said, "Why you limping?" and I said, "We played Leigh on Saturday. I went over on my ankle. He asked, "Did you win?" and I said, "Yes, mate". Then he said, "Did you score?" and I said, "Don't I always, pal?" and he laughed and said, "I will be coming next week as you're at home. These chisels are £48 plus vat." I said I couldn't pay that for them so he said just to leave them and he would put them back later. I limped out to the van and had to remove the level and hammer just to let me climb into the van.

I have to put this in to show you how stupid some people are. One of the lads in the pub kept asking me for a job. I asked him what he could do and he said, "Roofing, flagging, pointing and any manual work," so I said I would get him something. A couple of weeks later, we were doing a dormer house conversion to make the bedroom bigger because the bloke was in a wheelchair; absolute lovely man. He was a wagon driver and another wagon hit him head-on doing the same speed - 65 miles per hour. The other driver was drunk and he was fucked. It was planned to have a lift fitted so he could get upstairs, so I gave this lad a chance as there was some of the extended bedroom floor to go down and roof tiles to cut and a long slow rising ramp made with flags so he could get in the front door. This lad's name was Baz and on day 1, I said, "Do you fancy cutting the tiles and finishing the roof?" This was no problem so off he went. I was in the new extended bedroom, when next thing, bang! Baz comes through the roof and he has two legs sticking through. We got him out, then I said, "Why not have a smoke on the roof to chill you out?" So, I went downstairs and I was talking to the owner who was watching cricket on the tv. I went in and asked if he would like a brew and he said yes so, I made 3 coffees and 2 cups of tea and two rounds of toast for the homeowner. I took them in with his coffee and put them on the tray on his wheelchair. He thanked me and was telling me about this player who was bowling. I didn't know about cricket but you have to look interested, so I shouted upstairs, "Lads, your brews are here!" A couple came down and next thing, a big bang and Baz had come through the ceiling above the television! There were now three of us in the living room with the homeowner, this time only one leg, but I was fucking fuming and the lads had to go back upstairs to get him out. He kept saying sorry and he said it that many times I had to tell him, "If you say it again, I will knock you out; go away." So, it all got cleaned up and we patched it ready to make good and I said to Baz, "Can you take those bags of plaster upstairs, please?" So, he picked up a bag of board finish, took it up to the landing then balanced it on the banister and before I could say 'get that off', it split in half and half the bag peeled open and covered the bloke in the wheelchair in the hall! I felt like crying! I lost it completely. I ran upstairs, got him by the throat and said, "You get this house back to how it was before. Don't say sorry, just sort it!" I was in the bedroom with the joiner and he said, "Have you seen what he is doing? You really need to see this." When I looked over the banister, he was hoovering plaster powder off the bloke in the wheelchair with the hoover nozzle! I thought, 'I am going to fucking kill him!' The homeowner was so nice about it, but when we got done, I dropped Baz at home and he said, "What time tomorrow?" and I said, "Stay in bed; you're safer in there, mate", and drove off.

Me and my labourer ended up in a big college in Liverpool where they taught health and beauty. We were testing all their appliances, hair dryers, curling tongs, straighteners and anything else with a plug on it to make sure it was safe. One hell of a job! We sat at a desk and hundreds of girls aged 17 to 21 lined up to come to you. We would test the item and put a sticker on it for them. We were there for 3 days and when we got done, the main guy came over and said, "Thanks for that, lads. When are you doing the rest?" We asked him what he meant and he took us to this room, opened the door and it was full top to bottom with everything you could ever need if you were a hairdresser or nail person. So, we said we would start tomorrow. As we got there, I said, "Get my big toolbox and take everything out of it." so, we carried the toolbox and the tester to the room, then we printed a load of stickers off as these things were still boxed. I filled the toolbox up and walked down to the van to empty it, then walked back up again, filled it up and went back to the van. I did this about 6 times! We had all sorts and it was good stuff, but I had a wife and two girls, so I took it home and sorted mine out and my mates out as per normal. I gave everything away as I didn't like to sell things to people I knew when I had got them for free. I was even going to the people who supply me with goods and giving them whatever they wanted out of the van.

I did a lot of work for drug dealers, mostly renovating houses they had bought for cash. I worked for one lad who had to leave Liverpool and live in Burnley. He had a small family problem - he had shot his uncle and then, when they turned up at his house, they shot his mum so no love lost. I built a small hideaway on the bottom 4 stairs. I fitted hinges and you could lift up the carpet and the stairs lifted up and he would put a large block of cocaine in there the same size as a concrete block. But he always paid on time. One day I went, and the street was closed off by the police and I said, "I am working at house 24, mate", so they let me through and I banged on the door. His sister opened the door and we walked in. I said, "Where is he?" and she just walked off, so I got on with fitting the fire and plastering. When I went upstairs to the toilet, I could hear him calling my name and I said, "Where are you?" He unbolted the loft hatch and said, "Sorry, I can't come down. I stabbed a lad last night in the groin. Do me a favour - put some gloves on and take the knife, the balaclavas and the gloves out of that big pot boiling on the stove." I asked him why he was boiling them and he said it was to get rid of the DNA, so I went down, poured the water down the sink, cooled the stuff down, wrung it out and put it on radiators. Then, I put the knife back in the knife block, finished the job and then went home. Later on, I had been to the gym and I was lying on the bed and Crimewatch was on. He was on the list of Merseyside's most wanted men, so I rang him, and he said, "I have just had one call. I am getting out of here. I will ring you tomorrow off another phone". He had gone to Scotland but was sent down after a few months in hiding.

My next one had just done his house up and someone had set fire to it. I thought it didn't sound right as they had set fire to it twice in three nights, so I took a couple of men and it was a mess. He was only 21 years old, thin, nothing on him and he thought he was King Kong. Even when you talked to him, he would say, "Yes, we hit this place last night and took the driver hostage, emptied the trailer then locked the driver in the back, tied and gagged." I said, "What stuff did you get?" and he said, "Loads of computer stuff and pallets of laptops". I told him I would take four laptops off him and he said it would be no problem. The job was a rip-out, so I said as it was an insurance job, I would get started the next day to get it out of the way. We got back the day after and he said, "Do you know anyone who does glass?" So, I gave him my mate's name, then a few minutes later, my mate rang and said, "Can you measure the windows that are smashed?" so I said, "No problem. Stay on the phone." I measured up then gave him the sizes and he said he would be there before 5 pm.

We stripped out the fitted kitchen and put a new kitchen back and patched the house and re-painted it, then, as I was under the units bolting the worktops down, the kitchen door opened and our kid said to a guy, "You look a right dick head with that on," and the guy then closed the door, so I came out of the unit and said, "Who was that?" and he said, "That dick head dressed up!" Next thing, all hell let loose. They smashed up the bedrooms, the bathroom and started on the living room, so I rang the lad and said, "There is 5 blokes in your house smashing it up and we have nothing to defend my men with." He was only 8 doors down at his mum's and he said, "Just get out and get in your van and move out of the way." Then they all came out and ran across the road and jumped in a car, but the bonus was they didn't go back into the kitchen so all my work was fine. Now, you have to understand, the night before I started, he had already had bullet-proof glass fitted to protect us but didn't say anything about it until now, so when he asked about repairing the bedroom, the bathroom and the living room, I just said, "Mate, I don't do bedrooms, sorry." We went back on the Saturday morning at 5 am to tile the kitchen just so we could get away before dinner time. On the Sunday, I told his mate I would look at his kitchen for him, so we met him in Kirkby Liverpool and drove round these streets following him and finally turned left at a pub and into a cul-de-sac. I pulled up at the back of him and he ran to his house and pushed the door closed but we could push it open. As I was looking at the kitchen and drawing it all up, he kept standing near the living room wall and twitching the curtains and he kept peeking out, so after we were finished with the drawings and measurements, I said, "Tommy, that's us", and he said, "Hang on; just let this car turn round and go," so we waited, and the car stopped so we had to stand there for 15 minutes. Once it had left, I said, "Who was that, pal?" and he said, "I have had a bit of trouble with the gang that run the pub and they have tried to shoot me twice; that's why I ran in. And with you coming in a van, they may think I am transporting something. There is a van coming in now; if it drives to the top, you get out and into yours, then I will pull my car across so they can't get to you and then I will go back over the other side of the city." So, me and my mate walked out, calmly got to the van and I was out of there like a bat out of hell! I didn't look back, I didn't get chance to put seatbelt on, I just wanted off the estate and onto the main road, then my mate said, "Nice bloke. You got a price in your head?" and I said, "Yes!" I ripped it out of the book and threw it out of the window and said, "I have kids' mate".

Then I was trying for 4 months to get paid for doing the house up that had been burned down. The insurance company said, "We are voiding the claim as he did not put his criminal convictions on the sheet", so I rang him and said, "Mate, I am £13,000 out of pocket!" He told me to claim it from the insurance so I said, "They won't pay because you didn't put your convictions down. Fuck me, how many have you got?" and he said, "A few. I have been up for murder 3 times, found not guilty each time and a few for drugs." He said that he couldn't do anything about it, so that was one I had to take on the chin. The bonus was 4 weeks later, someone drove a 7.5-ton wagon through his garden wall and through the front of his house. It even knocked the stairs off the wall, then they drove a black taxi through his mum's front bay window and when he rang, I said, "Mate, it would be weeks, even months before I could help as I am working away!" I thought, 'Fuck you'.

My next one was a belting bloke; he was kind, helpful, do anything for you and helped you carrying stuff in and moving shit out. He was buying quad bikes from Sweden and Italy and they were coming strapped to pallets and each had a customs sticker on to say it had been stripped and searched so he used to laugh at it. I had known him since I was young and he was well known for some of the stuff he used to do in his past. But this one was just crazy as he was only making a small mark-up on the bikes. He had been doing it for around 5 years, then he got arrested and I didn't see him for a bit, and then I was at a rugby game and he was there. We started chatting and I was asking him what he was up to and why he had gone walkabouts, so he told me what they were doing was hollowing out the blocks on the euro pallet and putting a large bag of cocaine in each hollowed-out block, but it was done with perfection. So, I said, "What happened?" and he said, "Well, on one of the wagons, the bikes were stacked and customs got them off, checked the tank and tyres and strapped it back to the pallet, but one of the officers had seen a date printed on the pallet and he said they didn't make euro pallets until two years after that, so they took it back down and took the pallet apart and found what they had been looking for over the past 5 years". He had ended up doing four years for that.

One of the scams I really admired was run by an old rugby guy I played with. He used to take 4 drivers with him and go to this big local company at 4 am and sign in as agency drivers from Drive Force. Then they would all drive out in an HGV wagon - none of them had a driving licence - but they would drive for 5 hours and drop the trailer off to one guy who took anything that the rear trailer had on it. This was anything from tyres to tampons, but they got a set price for each one. They would back the trailer into a warehouse and check it for a tracker. Each of the wagons had trackers but they had a track blocker in each to scramble the signal. Then they would drive closer to the company and park the cabs outside on the main road at the rear of the company yard. A real driver would then take the keys in and throw them in the wagon key box on the floor. Now that took some bollocks. Then the loaders would get a key out of the box and walk along the line, pressing the key, and take it in for its next trailer. They were doing this for months and making a lot of money but they were putting the work in. However, that came to an end when the handovers were changed, and you had to sign the key back in, but this company had thousands of trailers so that's why it took a long time to pull it up.

One Saturday night after playing rugby, I was out with all the lads and we were all in town having a good night. Then this guy they called Harry the Hat came walking over with a few of his back up men. He asked if he could have a word in private, so we walked out to the rear yard of the pub and he said, "I need your help, mate. I have spoken to a few people and all have said your name. I have a few houses and, as you know, I grow weed." So, I said, "Why do you need me?" and he said, "The house in Wigan is empty but the people that were in it didn't pay any bills so the electric board have been in and they took away the main fuse and I can't get one anywhere." So, I said, "Is it an old Wylex Board with black fuses?" and he said yes. I said,

"If it is after 1960, you may pick one up off an old electrician or if it's before 1960, you may struggle, pal". He asked if I could have a look and see if I could help him as the house had all been done up and was ready for a new grow. He gave me the address and we met there on the Monday at 11am. It was a nice place, big old 4-bedroom terraced place with lots of space and a big kitchen. The place was empty but clean and ready for him to set up so I had a look but it was a really old board that couldn't be replaced. So, he said, "Can you work your magic?" and I said, "Are you paying today?" He told me, "I have an envelope here; if you can get my electric on today, you can take it". I said, "Harry, I have been ripped off before, mate," so he said, "Here, put the cash in your pocket and you can give it back if you can't get the power on. Could you also put in some more sockets on the wall for me?"

It took us about one hour to fit 16 double sockets and I cut the top 6 inches off the brush handle, I planed it down so it was the same size as the missing 100-amp fuse then cut a groove along it and taped a 6" nail to it round the middle. Our kid said, "Don't tell me you're going to put that in!" I got the thick rubber gloves out of the van and then I put the glove on my right hand and put extra electrical tape round each finger just in case. Then, I got on the steps and pushed it in and all the lights came on. Our kid said, "Mate, I thought you were going to end up across the other side of the room!" I tested all the sockets - they were fine and then I pulled the block back out and waited for him to get back. Harry came in and he had 3 of his men with him. He said, "How did you get on?" and I said, "Do you want to do the honours? You just put this block I made into that gap." He looked and said, "Fucking no way! I don't even want to be in the room when you put it in the gap!" He shot out of the room, then I went up the steps, put it back in and closed the door. I shouted him to come back in and I gave him a tester to plug into the sockets and all the tester lights came on and I switched all the lights on in the house. He said, "Tucker, you are unreal. A lot of people have said good things about you." I said, "Listen, I don't know how much you have put in this envelope but I am not one to rip someone off." I took it out and there was £1000 in it, so I took £400 and gave him the £600 back. He stood and looked at me and said, "Mate, what you have just done has gained my full trust in you and if I can ever do anything for you, just ask". I said, "I did before but you wouldn't put the block in!" and he laughed. I made him promise he would contact me day or night if he needed the block taken out as it could kill someone.

Harry was so grateful and said he owed me big time. Then he gave me a hug and I put my tools away and got in the van. He came out and knocked on the window, so I rolled it down and he said, "Mate, take the rest of this money. I make a lot of money", and I said, "Harry, like I said, I will not rip someone off. I will take from a big company but not your normal man." He said, "You are a sound man and it's a pleasure to call you a friend." It was about 4 months later when I saw him in town and he was with about 15 blokes, all bodybuilders. He shouted me over and got me to shake all their hands. He told them, "You will never meet a more honest, kind but bent person as Tucker", and they were all laughing. He put his hand in my pocket and said, "You made me a lot of money and I can't repay you, so have a drink on me." I said thank you and that I would get the lads a round, then I gave him a hug and went to the bar and got 6 bottles of beer for me and the lads. I took them over and said to them all, "When he turns round, lift the bottle and say cheers", so I shouted Harry, he looked over and all my lads lifted their bottles and shouted cheers and he put his thumb up and told us to have a good night. After that, we headed to the night club. I had forgotten about the money, but when I pulled it out, it was £600 and I said to the lads, "Rest of the night is on me", and we had a great time. I had made friends with one of the main men in my town. I saw him a few times and waved or hugged him and then just went with my friends, but he always had loads of people round him every time you saw him.

I was out one night with my wife, my best mate and his wife, and we were having some food. When it came to the end, I asked for the bill and the guy said, "It has been paid by the man on the big table at the back in the corner." So, I walked round and Harry was sitting there with all his gorillas and a few women. I walked up and said, "Thank you very much for that; it was very kind of you." He asked if I had a minute, so we ended up in the kitchen of the restaurant and he told one bloke to go out. He said, "You know what, Tuck? I have people hanging off me 24-7 because of what I do and you are the only person who isn't trying to get close to me. But you are very polite every time we meet." I said, "Like you said, I would class you as a friend, and again, if you wanted me for anything, I would always be there to help you out the best I could." Then he said, "What would you say if I said to you that I need £5000 by tomorrow dinner or someone said they will shoot me?" And I said, "In that case, I will meet you in the morning at 9 am and give you the £5000 to sort your problem out. Just tell me where to meet you."

Then he put his arms around me and said, "Mate, I am worth a lot of money and I don't owe anyone but what you have just said to me, well, all the people sat at my table that I will be paying for, none of them would have said what you said". So, I said to him, "Harry, do you need £5000 or not?" and he laughed and said, "You have gone to the top of my tree; anything you need, no matter how big or small, ring me and it will be sorted within the hour." I told him that I would always return the favour and we walked back out. He hugged me again and said to the people on his table, "Raise your glasses because you will never meet another person like this one. He is a diamond and I would pay him anything if he wants to join up with me, but I know he will refuse. He is the best man I have ever had the pleasure of calling a friend. Here's to my very good friend, Tucker!" and he hugged me again and I said, "Thank you, mate; have a good night", and he pulled me back and whispered in my ear, "These lot are wankers, mate. I wish it was me and you sat down," then he kissed me on the cheek and sat back down. I just said, "Have a good night, everyone, and H, if you need me, I am always close", and he waved. We did do business again a few times but it was for the same thing; to get his houses ready for his lads to set a grow up, but Harry always rang me and made sure I was ok. He said, "I would love you to take control of some of my stuff because I know I could trust you 100%." I said, "H, I will always do anything I can for you and I won't ever let you down, but I have my company to run and like I said, if you are ever stuck for money, I will always give you whatever I can get my hands on. You are a great bloke and a pleasure to have as a friend".

We did another couple of jobs for him, some at his own house which I would not take payment for and he lost it one day saying, "Why won't you take the money?" I said, "All my life, I have never charged family or friends for doing work for them and I am not going to start now", so I walked over and gave him a hug.

Then we got asked to do a barn on a farm in Lancashire, so I said, "Can we stay over in the farm or do we sleep in the van?" and he said, "No, the house is fully furnished. I will stock the fridge and leave you beers. How long will you be?" I said it may take two days or even three as we needed to dig a trench from the house to the barn, and he said, "You just do what you need to do, pal". It took two full 12-hour days, so I said to the lads, "Do you want to stay over or go home?" They decided to stay over so we all had a shower, sat down with food and watched a DVD with a beer and had a laugh. I said, "Listen, tomorrow, clean the house and make the beds so it's all clean and I will pay you for the day." I spoke to Harry in the morning saying, "We are just finishing off and one of the lads is cleaning the house". When we met up and he paid me for the job, again, I gave him £500 back. He said, "What's that for?" and I said, "You have given me too much." He said, "I wish I had 10 of you; my life would be so much easier!" I said, "Mate, you know I am always there for you; just ring and I will be there." He said, "You did a great job and the fucking house has never been that clean!" I said, "I always clean up, mate", and he said, "You need to come and live with me!" and he gave me a hug. He had that barn running for 3-4 years until a couple of his lads drove to the barn to feed the plants with no road tax and got followed then pulled as the unmarked police car followed him for the last couple of miles and down the farm track. One had been smoking cannabis in the car. The police called for reinforcements and they searched the car and found a couple of mobile phones and the keys for the farm with the address written on the keyring, so they ended up searching the farmhouse, saw all the plant food, checked the barn and saw all the plants. They had got away with it for 4 years as they had insulated the barn goods well that the helicopter couldn't pick the heat up off the lamps through the barn roof.

The police had taken the mobile phones off the lads and found more inside the farmhouse so, after running all the checks on the numbers, that led them back to Harry as the main leader because all the calls on some of the phones were to and from him so he had no chance. He did fuck off to Spain to his villa but when he came back home, they chased him down the motorway and pulled him over, then he went on remand, then off to jail for 6 years, but he only ended up doing two years then he went back to Spain.

I then started working for a large company in Manchester. They were huge - a very big name. They also owned another 64 big brand companies that I can't name any for legal reasons but when I started there, they had me do a few jobs and some drains, then hang some doors, then changing lights. Now, I always took a lot of pride in my work and I also made anyone who worked with me do the same. I also insisted they left their work area spotless at the end, so this company loved me! They just kept giving me more and more work and the places were like Aladdin's cave; filled with everything you needed in your home. If I said something was nice, they would say, "I will sort you one out", and then you would have an item worth around £1400 free of charge; it was amazing. I started to look after the managers and pay them £100 to £200 a week and all they had to do, if a job was over £5000, was to make sure they let me know the other price before I submitted mine. Nest thing, the price came over as £4950 plus vat. I put mine in at £4046 plus vat, so I got the job. I think it cost around £400 for materials but again, they were made up, saying how neat it was and how clean the area was and how he had put all the work benches back in place.

The work was coming fast, and I was working 7 days a week. I didn't go on holiday and even worked some Christmas Days if I was needed. The place absolutely loved me; they couldn't do enough for me. They even gave me my own work area and an office so that I could do the estimates quicker for them. The only problem was the first year I paid around £65,000 in VAT but turned over £750k in one year, so I was shoving money all over the place. I wanted to get my VAT down and try to take some money out of the company so I priced a job on one of their other sites in Trafford and they wanted 350 metres of Armco fitting, so I got my mate to price fitting and I priced the barriers and legs and I was getting it to around £18000 but another company came in and priced against me and one of the managers sent it to me. They were at £45000! I thought, 'Fuck me' and I went in at £43500 and got the job. So, after the job was done, I still needed to get the VAT lower so I sat at the computer for hours making up invoices for the accountants. In all the years, they had never questioned any of the invoices, so I just kept quiet.

Ever since I had been a little lad, I had always saved money and, as I got older, I got better and better. So, when I was in my 30s, I was always having tattoos but all my tattoos had been drawn by me and meant something to me about my life. For example, I have a tractor with the number 4 in the big wheel because I was made to work on the farm when I was 4; I had an apple with books on because I was clever at what I did, and I had a man on a ladder cleaning the apple with number 8 on his back because I had my own window-cleaning round when I was 8 years old. Then I had a set of rugby posts and the crossbar had £1,000,000 on it and a man just about to kick the ball and that was because my aim in life was to be a millionaire someday. I also have a big old oak tree and when you look closely, the only thing on the tree is loads of branches; no leaves, and one owl and one magpie. The owl was because I was smart and always thought things through. Even if a plan went wrong, I always had a backup to cover myself if needed.

The magpie was because I couldn't go in anywhere without picking something up and 90% of the time, I didn't want it. I just gave it away to someone who needed it. I don't know why; it was just habit and I liked helping people, more so the people who came from the same area as me who had nothing because I started with nothing myself. So, after sitting down for a bit, I thought I could do this with every invoice I get - just pay the invoice cash, make a higher one and pay that into another account and give the receipt to my accountant. Anyway, I ended up with 24 different company invoices on my computer and I hammered it. Then came the time when I had no option but to put my money into stocks and shares. Even though I had started doing this when I was 18 years old, it was just a few hundred each month, or, if I made good money, I would put it all in there, but there was always plenty in the bank for the wife to waste on shite. Again, she didn't like me doing it, but loved spending it and was great at taking £300 to £400 to go shopping on a weekend. Not once, in all the years of marriage, did she come home and say, 'I have bought you this'. I even did my own washing and drying and there was only me in the house that could do any needlework as I had learned in Young Offenders.

So, now I was working on 5 of their sites across the north west and each site had something different, and I don't care who you are - no one could refuse to take stuff from the sites we were working on because it was everywhere - pots and pans, hair dryers, everything down to a dishwasher, so I sorted every one of my family out with stuff and all my friends. I would sort them out with stuff but I would never sell anything. I always gave it to them free of charge because it made me feel good that I was helping them out. I didn't need money; I got pleasure out of being thanked. At one point,

I couldn't cope with what money I was getting, but it put my kids through university, it bought their cars, it even bought them their homes. Now, not a lot of dads can say they have done that in their life. My wife wasn't happy that I gave them so much but I said, "I would sooner give it now when they need it and can use it to set themselves up than wait until when I die, and they don't need the help as they have scraped through life; that's what I did and I don't want them to do that."

By this time, my bill for paying all of the managers was hitting £1400 a month but I didn't care as I was getting everything. There were around 150 boxes outside and they said, "When you get the chance, can you put them in the skip with your fork truck at the weekend?" I said, "No problem", but when I opened the box, it was full of brass fittings so I put every box in my van and took them to a scrapman I know. I had to empty every box into a large bin, but I didn't mind, then I loaded the empty boxes back onto my van and went to the counter. He handed me £6200 and I said, "I hope you have given me a good price", and he said, "Tuck, I always give you good price." I asked him what I could do with all the boxes, so he said, "Just go round the corner; there is a cardboard place. Tell him I sent you." So, I drove round the corner and asked the guy if he could take the cardboard. He said, "Yes, it's clean; just throw the lot into this building." He wanted to weigh it to pay me for it but I said no, that he could keep the money for himself.

A few weeks later, one of the maintenance men said, "Do you mind taking some stuff to the scrapman? You will need to be careful", so I had to get my van between the two trailers so none of the cameras could see and then we loaded these tubes and bars into my van. Now, they were heavy and I had no idea what it was so I asked and he said, "It's nickel, so don't let him do you", so I went and spoke to the boss's son and they have a gun that tells you what metal it is so he puts it on. Next thing, 70% then he got a bin and we put it all in. I truly was thinking £300 to £400, but he wrote the weight down, I went to the window and his dad said, "You trying to kill me, Tuck?" He started laughing and said, "You need to come in, pal". So, I was let into the office and he bagged up £9400! I put it down the back of my pants and walked out, got in the van and drove off then I pulled over on the lay-by and got it out. I took £3000 out of it and changed the 9 to a 6 with some carbon copy I had got from the builders' yard, then I drove back and went in and said to the lad, "Here, that shocked me. You got £6400 for that load of shite!" He said, "Great; here, you take a thousand, I will take a thousand and we will tell them we got £4400 because none of them saw what went on." I stood outside thinking, 'did that really just happen'? Next thing, we were all sitting in the brew room with the £4400 and they gave me another £1100 so we all had £100 each. I got paid £850 for working there that one day as well - it was unreal. Then a couple of weekends later, one of the other guys said, "Come in our room for a brew about 9 am". I sat at the table and there were only two people in. I said, "Where are all the rest?" and they said, "We all went to a wedding last night and only us two made it in. Can you bring your van up to the top of the yard?" So, I said, "What about the camera in the corner?" and he said it was stuck and wouldn't move round, so I got the van and backed it up and they put in loads of that nickel again; pipes, corners, tubes, fittings and loads of bars. My van was on its arse and I said, "Look at my van! It should only carry 900kg." I took the van home and put nearly half of the stuff into my garage then took it to be weighed. We ended up with close on £6100 so I took the money in an envelope with the receipt inside and went into his office and said, "Everything is in here," and he opened it and said, "That's great!" I had asked for a receipt but he told me to burn it, then gave me £2000 and I carried on with my work. After they had left at 1pm, I took the van back up and there was loads of this stuff inside so I helped myself, but I put it all in cloth sacks, about 12 of them, and put them in the van with a couple of tubes and stored them in my garage.

The next time they asked me to take some they had a good stash and they loaded my van up. I drove to my mate's yard and went into the office. I checked with him that nickel was okay with him and he said it was. He said he would bring out a bin so I backed in, put it all in the bin and he put it on the scales. Back in the office, he said, "Come through, Tuck", and I walked to the back office. Fuck me, there was millions in this safe! He made me a brew then asked about my brother as he played rugby with him. I said, "He is fine. I will see him at the weekend", so he said, "Tell him I was asking and I said you're ok." He gave me £10,460 and I said, "Can you do me a favour and make the receipt for £7980?" and he said, "No problem, pal", so I drove back, went into the brew room and put the envelope down. Because I had said that the load was close to £8k, they didn't even check the receipt. They just asked, "How much do you want for taking it, Tuck?" and I said, "Just share", and they said, "You sure? You took all the risk." I said, "No, mate, a share is only right", so they gave me £2000 and I said, "Thank you. Let me know for the next one." They said, "Make sure it stays between us", and I said, "Mate, I promise; it's too good to fuck up!" So off I went with £4480 plus my £850 day's pay.

I went home and loaded all the nickel I had stored in my garage and drove to my mate's, backed in and there was a bin waiting for me. I loaded it up and brushed my van out into the bin and let him put it on the scale, then I went into the office for a brew with the boss and he said, "Are you splitting this?" I said, "Yes, there is 6 of us", and he said, "That was a good one that, pal. Do you want another receipt?" When I said yes, he gave me £14,895 and gave me another receipt for £10k. I didn't need it but I wanted him to think I was sharing it between 6 of us; it just looks better, so that one day, I took home £20,225 - not bad for a Saturday.

I had got some work to do for one of the lower-class drug dealers and he was okay but always moaned about costs and prices of stuff, so I never ever stole anything for him because he was ungrateful and wouldn't offer you anything if you did sort him out. We were re-plumbing the house and his mates would come and go all day but they were sound to get on with. Paulo was one he had met in prison, but he was a great lad and a good laugh. We even went for a drink with him. I don't know if he was Polish or Slovak but he was a top bloke. Anyway, a couple of months after, I was working in Wigan and we were late finishing, so I said to the lads, "Get done tonight save putting all the tools in the van and locking up, then getting them out tomorrow. I will pay you for the full weekend and you can have both days off." They all agreed.

Now, it was getting to midnight and we had finished, and the lads were cleaning up. I said, "I am just going to the cash point to get some more money", as I only had £2000 on me and I needed another £300. So, I went into Hindley and I remembered there was a cash point on the corner as I had been into the shop for milk and coffee, so I parked up and walked round and there was a BBQ gas bottle with the pipe going inside the cash machine. I thought, 'What the fuck?' then someone shouted my name. I turned round and it was Paulo. He said, "Come here", so I walked to him. He said, "What are you doing?" and I said, "I just need a few hundred to pay the lads". He said, "This one is not working" and I said, "It did the other day!" He said, "No. I make it not work. Go down the road; there is another at the post office", so I walked round the back to get in my van. Then, out of nowhere, there was a huge bang like a bomb had gone off so I got in the van and as I drove to the front, there was a big hole in the wall, the cash machine was in the middle of the road and these guys were just bagging all the notes floating about and two of them were stripping the cash machine! I thought, 'Fuck me, I have just worked like a pig all week and they got that out in ten minutes'. So, I went to the other machine and got back to site. I didn't say anything to the lads; we just loaded up and I paid everyone and then gave them the weekend off and the next day, me and my brother-in-law went onto the next job and put up all the palatine fencing to keep people away from the concrete we had to dig up over the next week. I had to go into a different part of the works - it was a building for Quality Control, and I was doing some toilets, a couple of sinks and some drawers in two of the offices. So, when I got into the office, there was a room at the end, so I took the drawers out, did the repairs and left them on top on the desk as that is where they had been left for me. I put all my stuff away and went back in and walked into this room. It had everything in it, all boxed up; big orange pots for making stew in the oven, so I took 9, that was 3 of each size, and put them in the van. I also got a couple of boxes of pans, a couple of kettles and 2 toasters. I then locked up and drove to security as you had to give your pass in and sign out. I had a chat and watched tv with him for a bit then I said, "That's me, pal. I will see you tomorrow." I got home and put the stuff in the garage, and the wife got home about 5 pm. I said, "Oh, there is some stuff in the garage; let me know what you want or don't want and I will give the rest away". She went in and came back with one of the pots and said, "Do you know how much these cost? They are close to £500 each!" and I said, "Well, there is a set for your mum and one for your brother", and she said, "No, don't give all of them away. Just give Mum a couple and my brother a couple". I didn't care what she did, I just needed them out of the garage.

Next day, I went into work at 7.30 am, had a brew with security, then went about my job list. I decided to go back and get a set each for a couple of my mates, but then everyone started asking me to get them stuff, and like a fool, I would do it and drop it off. When they said, "What do I owe you?" I always said, "Don't worry, I didn't pay for it so I can't charge you; that wouldn't be right." The more I got people, the more other people asked, and then some would ask for big things like range cookers and American fridge freezers and it was hard because they were stored in two different warehouses. These took a bit longer to get.

One of my main jobs was repairing pipelines while they were still fully active, so, if there was a leaking gas main coming from the oil refinery and running under a canal, we would locate the leak and we would fix it while it was still leaking. I worked at a couple of the big oil refineries doing this. It was hard work and long days and the money wasn't as good as doing it for the place that owned all the companies because they would send me to London, Blackburn, Wales, Staffordshire, Manchester or Liverpool but we did do a lot in Slough and Wimbledon. They paid all your costs from fuel to food to parking and hotel and expenses for food and drink. I wasn't a lover of working away from home because I used to worry about my youngest girl as my wife used to treat her like shit and I was always scared she may harm herself. She was also bullied at school so she was getting it from all over the place. I wished I could just take her and set up home on our own. Also, the money was great but there was no side-line; you couldn't get any stuff from the sites. While I was working in Slough, it was a Saturday and we were going to work till 6 pm, do all day Sunday and finish Monday, but I rang my youngest girl and she was upstairs upset, so I stayed on the phone with her. I was fucking fuming inside! Anyway, I said, "You watch tv and I will ring you when I get to the hotel". I told my mate and he said, "What do you want to do?" so I said, "Work today till midnight, go to the hotel, come back at 6 am Sunday and get it finished and I will pay you an extra £500 cash." So, he said, "You're the boss", so I rang my little girl about 8 pm and spoke to her for a bit and said, "Listen, I am going to work late so I can get home tomorrow night". She was so made up! I said, "Put your phone under your pillow and I will message you when I finish". Anyway, it was 12.30am when we wrapped up. I had huge blisters on my hands and knees so my mate drove to the hotel and I messaged my little one but she didn't come back until morning, around 8.30, saying 'sorry I was asleep I miss you'. We had started work at 6.30 am, so I messaged her back and said, 'keep out of the way and do your homework. I will ring when I leave', and she said, 'Ok I love you'. That killed me as I wasn't with her.

So, I said to my mate, "Don't stop, just keep that stuff coming", and we ended up finishing around 2 pm. I was covered in shite, so, we had these wipes to get clean but they burned hell out of the blisters on my hands, so we just threw the stuff in the van and I drove home. I got home for around 5.50 pm and I got out of the van, walked through the garage, put all my clothes on the floor and went into the house in my underpants. I kissed the wife, kissed my oldest and gave the kids £50 each and my youngest came upstairs with me. She used to sit on the toilet and talk to me while I was in the shower. I asked her, "Is everything okay? You didn't get told off for nothing?" and she said, "No, everything is good and better now you're back". That's why I didn't like working away.

Loads of people offered me work doing up country homes but you had to live on site for 6 months. One guy offered me work and when I asked how much, he said, "£200 a day". I said "If you would have said £500 a day, I may have done a couple of weeks for you, but no thanks, I am fine". He said, "There is only you I know who can make good old coves and make flowers and petals out of plaster and stick them on after," and I said, "I may catch you on one of the pub renovations". All the old pubs had ceiling coves with curved leaves and roses so that was the stuff I liked. Also, people in big houses got to know and they would stand and watch me working. I worked at the home of a spinal surgeon and his wife, who was also a doctor, and I was doing a repair to a cove about 2 metres long. He asked if he could help as he loved stuff like this, so I took the damaged piece down, salvaged what I could to stick back up and cleaned it all down. I made my own Stiptex that an old-time plasterer had shown me. I brushed it onto the laths and walls then started to build up the base, only mixing a double handful each time then letting that set before going again. He said, "How do you do those roses and curved petals?" so, I said, "Give me 20 to build this up and I will show you!" He went to have his tea, and when he came back, I had a couple of roses on my board setting and was curving some open leaves over rolled-up newspaper. He just stood there quietly then said in a posh voice, "Fuck me, you're amazing! The skill you have is outstanding". I said, "It was only what I was taught. There is some stuff on the board - flatten it with the trowel, nice and easy like buttering bread", but he was a little heavy-handed, so I mixed the stuff thicker and added cement and said, "Now, you have to work quicker; you only have around 4 minutes with the cement in". I cut out a leaf for him using my small tool then I left it on the board andsaid, "Now, put the spine down the leaf and cut from the middle out". Once he had done that, I opened it up for him, then I said, "Now, turn the tool round, slide under the leaf and sit it on that roll of newspaper". He did it and he was made up so then I showed him how to make petals and build a rose. He said, "This is better than sex!" and laughed. I said, "Make a brew, then we will dress the cove in about 10 minutes", so he and his wife had tea with me, and they just kept looking at the coving. Then I started to dress it with some slip as glue and brushed it round. With the roses, I stuck toothpicks in them to hold until they had dried, but I had pushed them in far enough that I could cover them. I wet the slip down and went over the full length of cove to make it look like one new length, cleaned up and put my stuff in the van. It was 10 o'clock at night, but the bloke was over the moon. He said, "I have guests coming tomorrow", and I said, "Don't forget to tell them you did the second rose and the next 2 leaves!" He said, "I don't know how to thank you. How much do I owe you?" I said, "I told you £80 to £100, so just give me £50 as you helped". He said, "I really like you; you're a very kind person. I would have paid £800 to £1000 to get that done", and I said, "Yes, but he may not have done it right and had no pride in his work". He said, "I can see how much pride you have; you even cleaned the full room and wiped all the walls down. I told you to leave it for us". I said, "I can't leave a job untidy; it's not right on the customer". He walked over, gave me his card and £100 and I said, "I tell you what, I will take £60".

He said, "I can't tell you how much work you will be getting as I have friends in high places", so I said, "Thank you, if I need help to get work, I will give you a call, but you will be waiting a long time for me to call!" He came over, gave me a hug and said, "Thank you so much. You have just amazed both me and the wife. Don't get me wrong, it wasn't for the money, but the challenge. I knew it was hard to do and everyone loved to watch you, even more when you let them get involved."

To be truthful, I didn't want the extra work as I was making more money working for the larger companies. When I had done work for the large manufacturer, the money was crazy! I was doing some work and then earning £10k to £14k on a weekend, but the thing was, I always had lads who would drop everything for me because I paid very well so they didn't mind working over the Christmas Holidays and Boxing Day as I was paying £100 a day and that was in the late 1990s to 2000. I didn't mind myself because the money was more than a barrister was getting, but I had to get the VAT down. In my first year, I think I paid around £62,000 in VAT and around £10,000 in corporation tax so, I needed to do something about this. At first, I just started to pick up receipts from outside B&Q, but I then got a receipt from a company and it was all wet and ripped as I had it in my work pants, so when I got home, I used to spend 4 to 6 hours on my computer typing estimate invoices and RAMS up and sending them into the company. so, I thought, 'I will go and see the manager of this supplier and try to do a copy of this invoice', so I started to ask each manager of each supplier to sort me some invoices out and I would pay them because I needed the company logo and the address. It took me a few weeks to talk to all my suppliers but they were all great. Each one would give me an invoice and I would just give him a few hundred pounds and put the invoice into my accounts and claim it back through work so it showed I was using 50 to 60 times more materials than I was originally ordering, but my accountant thought I was just busy at work.

At month's end, I took my accounts in and nothing was said, so I thought, 'If this can be accepted by an accountant, I wonder if I could do anymore and do the payment to my wife's bank so my cheque stub would match with the receipt?' so I wrote one for around £10,200 including VAT and paid the cheque into the wife's bank account and it started from there. I was spending my free time on suppliers' sites and redoing their invoices. Some had lines down, some had price boxes in; it just took time to do. I had one supplier that never charged me anything as I used to supply them with stuff from work. To be truthful, there weren't many places where I used to pay for stuff as I supplied everyone with free stuff from work. At this one company, my good mate worked there so stuff was free anyway, and I got a load of their own receipts from him. They were blank and you had to true the page lengthways along the dotted line, and it had boxes in and a box at the bottom for the total price. This was a bastard to do! I must have used 30 blank white paper sheets, then printed and lifted it up to the light and they were a couple of millimetres out, so I ended up dropping the font size and lifting it up two lines and it hit the box bang in the middle! I was made up because it took so long. Now I could start to use up what I had. I was putting them in for around £2600, anything up to £7800 but I never went over that cost. It was the bigger companies I would put in for around £30,000 up to £42,000 but they all had to be different fonts and with the VAT on so I could claim the VAT back. This cut things down till I was getting a VAT return of over £4000 but then my accountant, who was an old friend, called me in and said, "Mate, I have just clicked what you're doing because you missed the receipt in the cheque book". He had all my stuff on the meeting table and he said, "Please tell me, as I have just got one of each company you have put in and there is 18 of them. How many of these are real?" I said, "The truth doesn't leave this room; probably one or two". He said, "Fuck me, pal, so how many companies have you got that you print off your own computer?" I said I was not sure, but it may be over 30. He said, "You can go to jail, pal. What the fuck is going through your head?" and I said, "Mate, I work 7 days a week, I don't drink, I don't smoke, so fuck it. I want to earn some money". He told me I was playing with fire, so I said, "Okay, mate, I understand, but you will still be getting a couple". He said, "A couple is fine; just fucking 18 a month is wrong! Now, fuck off and try to do a couple of months free of these."

I was working in Staffordshire and I got on tops with the boss. I was giving him more and more cash - some months, £2000, but it was flooding back in work. I said to him, "What do I do now?" He said, "Send me 2 invoices, both under £1000", so it was great. Then I started to get on with the lads in the warehouse. There were only around 8 on each shift so I got to know them all and I would sort stuff for them to keep them on side. I would buy breakfast for everyone; it cost around £40 so it was nothing. One of the lads came up and said, "Tuck, can you do me a favour?" and I said yes. He said, "Can you drop a couple of boxes of Tefal pans off at my mate's?" So, I said, "Yes, just put them in the back of the van". He gave me directions to get to his mate's unit and when I got there, I said, "Order to drop some pans?" and he said, "Just back in here, mate", so I got out, opened the back door and thought, 'What the fuck?' He had put two pallets in, so we had to unload then go and get the food. I took the box into the office staff and the other to the lad's brew room and said to him, "You got a minute, mate?" and he came outside. I said, "What the fuck are you doing? There was two pallets! You need to get those pallets out of my van and get rid of the wrap off them". He said, "No problem. Do you want any?" There was me and my labourer so I said, "Put me a couple in, please", then we drove home. I backed down my drive, opened the back doors and thought, 'Shit! He has done it to me.' He had put two fucking pallets in my van, 20 boxes on a pallet and two boxes of pans in each box. So, I drove round to everyone I used for materials and gave them all a set of pans. They were all made up. I gave them to the in-laws, everyone, even my family, and I gave the wife some for her friends at work/ We didn't keep any at home because I didn't want anything at my house, but everyone was made up with me. I must have had 20 to 30 phone calls a day asking for something. In the main warehouse, they had around £800 million pounds worth of stock. The place was huge! It was close to 400 metres long and 300 metres wide with loads of racking on all three sides of the building. There was a warehouse manager they called him Monk because he looked like Little John from the film Robin Hood and he was huge into his Rugby League so he loved me. I softened him up with some stuff from some ex-player mates of mine. I was 5'8" and he was close on 6', just under, but he was about 22 stone, so I had to allow for that. I gave him some training stuff. He also loved Warrington and I had a couple of friends who played there so I called in a couple of favours and sorted them with stuff from work. I got him a framed shirt signed by the team and put it up in his office one weekend when he was off. On the Monday, he rang me and said, "I don't know what to say", and I said, "Look in your top drawer". I had put 6 tickets to the next home game in an envelope and he said, "Mate, I must owe you something", and I said, "It's fine, pal. If I need anything, I will always ask you." I was getting really close to him. Then, the next weekend, he was going the game and I had got him tickets to get him into the players' lounge afterwards so he could take his wife and kids and his Mum and Dad. So, on the Friday, I was on site and he was all over me, but I didn't ask for anything. We just chatted all morning and I left around 1pm as I was going to the other site. He rang me again and said, "Mate, thank you so much for this; the family are buzzing about it".

I said, "Have you been in your drawer in the office?" and he said, "No,

I am sat there now; why?" and I said, "I have put some beer tokens for the bar in an envelope for you so you can have a drink". In the envelope I had put £400 and a note saying, "I couldn't get the tokens - use this as it will pay your taxi there and back to enjoy, mate." Anyway, a few minutes later, he rang and said, "Mate, you don't have to do this", and I said, "Listen, pal, you look after me with work and anything I need so I want to look after you, so, the least I could do is sort you and the family a day out. Just go and enjoy the day, mate; see you next week".

After that, I went to the site in Blackburn and sorted the list out that I had been given for the weekend. I started it on Friday as they finished at dinnertime and worked until 7 pm then drove home to watch the rugby at 8 pm. I was back there on Saturday, and I had finished everything by dinner time so I said to my mate, "Stay in the van and sit in the driver's seat", so security would think I was in the van. The cameras were shit but I had seen something earlier in one of the offices so went back in to check it out. There were about 30 large boxes of B&O DAB radios and each box had 6 radios in. Now, I am not stupid - I know what these are worth, so I took two boxes, and re-arranged the rest, even replacing the boxes with something else in a box at the bottom. The ones I put in place were not as big but I moved them to the front so you would only see when you had got to the bottom. Then I put the radios in the back of the van. I said to the lad I was with, "Here, mate, I will pay you for all day. I have put some radios in the back. Do you want a couple?" He said, "No thanks, I never use the radio". My next stop was security, and I went in and gave them some cakes I had got the day before and said, "Come on, let's have a brew", and we sat and had a cake with them. One of them asked, "Are you in tomorrow?" I said, "To be truthful, I should be in, but I have finished all of my work so there is nothing left on the sheet. That would mean me driving here and walking round all day just to show I have been on site". He said, "You don't have to do that; no one is in so I will just put you down as coming in. When you sign out, sign again below and leave it. If someone comes in, I will say you signed by mistake." I was really grateful so I sent my lad to the van and when he was doing the dishes, I went into the kitchen and put £50 in his back pocket and said, "Get yourself a bottle of wine on your way home and I will catch you in the week. My phone is on if you need me", so I left the site and then headed south to get home. As we got on the motorway, my phone rang and it was him. He said, "What are you doing? Wine is only £6!" I said, "Sorry, I meant get yourself a case", and he laughed and said, "I owe you one for this", and I said, "Don't worry, you help me enough. Just have a good weekend." All I was doing was priming him up to get him on my side. That meant I could go and do a private job the day after, so it ended up with 4 of us doing a kitchen fit in one day. We got done around 8 pm then went for a pint. It was a good way to get paid twice - once for the kitchen, £400 cash, and £820 from a job in the factory I wasn't at that day, so it was a good weekend because I cleared over £2600 for 2 days. I gave the wife £100 and £50 to each of my two girls and that kept everyone happy. I know I was working a lot but I did have a goal to hit.

I had put 4 range cookers in my van and dropped them off and went back. I had picked food up so all the lads were eating, then he came back in and said, "Can you drop them off, pal?" I said, "Mate, you're going to get me shot!" So, I dropped them off, came back and got my work done. He came over and said, "Can I have a word, Tuck?" So, we went into the toilets - it was more private as there were no cameras in there - and he said, "Take this, mate, thanks", and I said, "I am okay. I don't want anything, pal. I don't mind doing the odd one for you". We swapped numbers, then, when I had got home later, he rang and said, "I put you a drink in your glove box. You okay for doing a couple more?" so I said I told him there were only three security men I trusted so he said, "You say the word and I will make them disappear." I went out to the van and got the envelope out of the glove box, took it into the house and opened it. There was £2000 in it and I thought, 'Last thing I need is more money'.

I had hit a point that both my safes were full and I needed to get rid, so one night when we went out for some food, we decided that we would move. I said, "You do know I have just spent £12,500 doing the full downstairs up and now you're asking about moving to a new house! Fuck, why didn't you say that before I did all this work?" And she said, "It's up to you". The kids were saying, "Go on, Dad, get a nice big house", and one was up for sale, so I did a deal. He was getting my house and £130,000 and we shook hands. I didn't tell the wife and kids. I waited a couple of days as I told him get a solicitor and we would use the same one so when he said it was all sorted, a letter came to mine two days later. One of my daughters' friends was having tea with us, so I stood up, went into the kitchen and got a bottle of champagne and 5 glasses, went into the dining room, popped the bottle, filled each glass and gave them one each. The wife was looking at me strangely, then she said, "What are you doing?" I said, "Right, I want you all to raise a glass and toast with me", then I put the letter on the table and said, "To our new home!" and they were all screaming. She was hugging me she was so excited and when I sat down, she said, "Are you joking?" I said, "No, but you need to get your skates on as I have told him I want to swap homes in 10 days' time". She said, "Oh, my god! I can't believe it - we are going into a big detached house. What about the mortgage on ours and the new one?" I said, "I paid our home off last year; the new one is sorted. I am paying cash so no mortgage." A few days after, I went round and gave him £130,000 in cash in a carrier bag and said to him, "Do you want to count it?" and he said, "Do me a big favour; come to the bank with me", and I said, "I can't be seen in a bank with that type of money", and he said, "No, just for protection to get me into the bank!" When we got there, he went inside, and he was gone for about 30 minutes. When he came out, I said, "What the fuck have you been doing?" and he said, "They had to count it, mate", so I dropped him off at what was my house. I spent a lot of time doing work to the house and building a brick summer house in the garden and a full-size orangery on the back but, as I was at work every day, I had to flood it with men as I like stuff done quicker. I was there for the main stuff; the drains and the concrete and I let the brickies build it while I was working in the warehouses, but the good thing was, all the materials I just booked to my sites so work paid for everything including the lads' wages. I was getting to drop stuff off for the lad in Staffordshire, I then altered all the plumbing and did the re-wire myself, dry-lined the walls, boarded the ceilings and skimmed the full room out over two nights. One night. I was so late that I got a shower at 1.15am and was going to work the next day at 7 am but I was hooked by what I was making every week. My stuff at home was all built and paths down, decorated and carpets down in 6 weeks, so not bad going. After this, I had to concentrate on moving money from my company and making my receipts match up to my cheque book. I was getting better and better at this all the time.

We did a job for a company in Runcorn, and they wanted 300 metres of double-height Armco Barriers fitted, so I got my friend who was a steel fabricator to price the job and I priced up the Armco with a couple of companies. My mate said, "Around £6800 to fit, mate,", and the barriers were costing me £13000, so I had a price of around £25,000 plus VAT in my mind. I spoke to one of the site managers as he was a friend of my brother's and he said, "I will have a look for you if I get chance. Have you got a price?" I said, "I am waiting for the Armco price to come back". after the next day, he said, "There is a company that does the motorway works and their price is £62,000", so I said, "That's good. I thought I was expensive until you told me that, but the barriers are very costly", so I went back with a price of £59,680 to supply and fit. No sooner had I sent it than I got a reply; "Can you book the job asap?". I ordered the barriers to be dropped at the site and the invoice sent to my email, then I booked my mate and his team for the weekend. I got an email saying the barriers would be there on the Wednesday and these two wagons pulled up and they were unloaded, and I thought, 'Fuck, no wonder it cost that much; there is loads!' The lads came and fitted it in the two days, so he rang and said, "There is a load of Armco left over", and I said, "Yes, I got extra", which I hadn't. I rang the company and said, "Can you pick the stuff up that we didn't use as they changed the size of the job?" She said, "No problem, but you will have to pay £95 for collection". Once it had been collected, she said, "I will alter your invoice and send you the refund", so I said, "Sorry about this but the drawings didn't take account for the diesel tank, so we only put 150 metres up". She then sent me a new invoice for £7800 and I asked my mate what I owe him. He said, "£4000 cash or £6000 on a cheque", and I said, "See you in ten minutes with cash", so the job cost me £12000 and all I did was order the stuff and send some back. I had been paid all of £72,000 for a £12000 job so, every night, when I came home from work, I would sit at the computer typing this bill, changing the font, putting the weight of the stuff, the price of each item including the nuts and bolts and there were 4 sacks of them. Everything had been galvanised too, so I got my invoice for the stuff at just over £52k with the VAT. I also printed another to match what I had paid before the £7800 so they both looked the same. I did the large bill two days before the smaller one so I could say they asked for more and I did both of the cheque stubs to Armco and one of the cheques to the account I had set up in my mate's name. This was the account that I used to pay money into the stock market, but I always left around £30k in just in case I needed it.

However, by this time, I had gone past the million pounds I always wanted to have, plus other money in other banks and cash at home to pay the labourers. I thought I would feel different and everything would change but it didn't and by this time, I had stopped drinking too as I was travelling to work at 5 am and I didn't want to lose my licence because I would have lost my contracts. I came home one Sunday around 2 pm and I had done my paperwork the night before, so, I just had a shower and put my shorts and vest on. I liked to sit on the stairs at the bottom as I used to do this when I was young, and I would do it when I was working out a price for a job. I had opened the post from the day before and there were a few bank statements in there. When I looked at them, I realised I had over £150k in the banks, plus £40k in the safe and over a million in stocks and shares. Also, my house was worth £420,000 so on paper, really, I was worth close to £1.6 million. I didn't really think about the house and all the other stuff. I had been killing myself just to make a million and I had made it a couple of years ago, so then I thought I would up my game. I want to hit £2 million by the time I am 50 years old, but no one had a clue. I didn't have anything flash. I never bought new clothes, but I did buy designer from eBay, only the best stuff. Even though my wife was buying herself loads of stuff every weekend, I always kept a tight rein on my money because I needed to pay people off and this would make me more 'speculate to accumulate', so I always made sure I had a minimum of £400 in my work pants just in case I needed to pay someone or one of the managers on my payroll that was getting bigger every month.

It's strange as I look back- I always saved and had money, but I got pleasure out of giving it away because the person you would give the money to was really in need of it, so they were all over you and said nothing but nice things about you. My wife didn't like me giving it away, even when I first put money into stocks for both my kids. She went mad, but I said, "Fuck off, it's money and the kids will need it soon". But she knew I would not let the kids touch it. I would always give them cash whenever they asked, even if they were going out with their friends, I would give them £100. The wife would say, "Why have you given her so much?" and I used to say, "You never know how much you need when you're out". She never complained if she was going out with her friends and I would give her around £120; she just said 'thank you, love' and off she went. Next day, my kids would offer me the money they had left and it could be £80 to £100 but I always said to them, "Put it in your purse, love; you may need it in the week".

Another good week was when I went back up to work at the site where The Monk was manager. He was all over me, so I had taken two lads with me to do the lights so I could go and have a brew with Monk. He said, "Mate, thank you so much for that the other week; the wife and kids loved it". I asked him, "Did a couple of the players come to you in the bar?" said he said, "How do you know?" and I said, "I was out with them the night after. I had asked them to look for you and the family". Then he said, "Fuck me, who don't you know?" and I said, "No one, mate, but I like to keep close to my friends". For the first time, he asked if I needed anything off site and I said, "No, mate, I am good thanks, but if you need me to drop anything off for you, I pass your house on the way home". said he said that would be great. I told him the van was empty so I could take anything for him. So, he asked, "How the fuck do I get one of those SMEG American fridge freezers out?" and I said, "Just put it in loading bay 30". Bays 30 to 35 had doors on the outside so you could reverse the van in and that is what I used to do to let them get used to me parking under the bay. I told him just to leave everything he needed stacked up against the wall, then I went off to join the lads. Later, I opened Bay 30 and fuck me, he had put everything there as he was having a new kitchen and he didn't miss anything, but the lads were a little set back. They said, "What if he is testing you or lining you up for a stop on the way out?" and I said, "I don't think so, but we can do a trial run", so I backed under for 20 minutes and then drove out. I stopped at security, got out and said, "I won't be long; just going to B&Q", and they lifted up the barrier, so I drove out and went round to the butty shop and got the food in. I dropped some with security and some with the lads and I sat with Monk and had mine in his office with a brew. He said, "This is the list of items I put in the bay. I was going to buy them with my discount" and I said, "Well, you can save that for another time." He said, "I will pay you for taking them", and I said, "No, mate. I can't take money off friends; that's not me". He was panicking a bit saying, "I hope no one saw me, and what if you get stopped?" and I said, "You have another brew and let me worry about that". So, we finished our work, loaded up and off we went. I backed down his drive and took the stuff round the back and I said to his wife, "He is sorting his discount at work. I just saved him £30 on delivery." She thanked us and we stacked most in the dining room and the rest in his garage. Then we said goodbye and drove off home. as soon as I got home, I rang Monk and he said, "Are you ok? Have you left?" I said, "Mate, calm down; you will have a heart attack. I have just dropped the lads. All your stuff is in your house and garage." Then he said, "Tuck, I have never met anyone like you. Thank you so much and I will make you some money next week". The next week, we were up there for 3 days as they wanted extra labour to clear some stuff out. When we got there, the big boss said, "Listen, I have spoken to Monk and he is going to need your advice." When I got to Monk's office, he said, "We are clearing a load of old stock out as you have to keep spares for 6 years, so we need to clear all the racks of old stock." Then he said, "Come and look at this!" He took a box and opened it and it was full of brass fittings. I asked how many boxes he had, and he said 30 pallets. I said, "Right, double up a load of 4 pallets into my van," then we went to the scrap place close by and I got just on £12000 for them. As I was driving back, I realised he wouldn't have a clue, so, I had a note pad and I put down '4 pallets £4600' and went in and said got another load. Off I went back and dropped the same and came back and, on my pad, I put '2nd 4 pallets £4200'. We ended up loading 5 runs as that was all we had time for, and I had on my pad a total price of £26,060 and took this cash into his office. We split up the money, then I told him to get the other 10 pallets and hide them so no one saw them then we could do the same tomorrow. So, just that one day made me around £48,000, the Monk got £10,000 and his boss got £6,000 and they were made up. Monk said, "Mate, I have never had hold of so much money in my life", and I said, "Stick with me - we can make it bigger". after the next day, I took the other 10 pallets and cleared £34,000 and took back £14,000 to him. said he said, "You take £10,000 and I will have the £4000", and I said, "No, mate. We have £7,000 each; it's your stuff." I asked him what else was on the list and that day and the next day, we pulled out brass, copper and aluminium. I took the lot in and made another £30,000, while Monk ended up with another £6,000. I was very convincing when I got back and by splitting the chuck the couple of days before, I had his full trust by then, but he did okay. It paid for getting all his home done and he bought a new car and he said it was all down to me.

So, you can see I was pulling money from all places and don't forget, I got paid through my company over £6000 with the VAT for me and the lads for 3 days but that was because the boss had also had a cut. I sat with Monk and he said, "If you ever need anything, just tell me what and what colour and I will get it for you", and I said, "Mate, I am sound; if I need anything, I just take it off the racks when you're all on break and put it in the van!" He said, "Fuck me, so that's where they are going!" and started to laugh. I said, "Listen, that's not where they are going but if I tell you, it stays with me and you." He agreed, so I told him that one of the lads had asked me to drop something off for him and I did, then he asked me to drop some cookers off at the same place and when I got back, he gave me £2000. He said, "Who was it?" and I said, "Mate, we said we wouldn't say who it was, but I have dropped stuff for everyone". Monk went quiet and I said, "Sorry if it pissed you off, mate. I won't take anything for him again", and he said, "Please don't", and I promised I wouldn't. Then he told me, "You can do it", and I said, "Are you sure?" and he said, "Yes. You have his buyer so can you go and see him? But he can't tell the person that you are supplying". So, I said, "I will go and see him when I go to the butty shop", and he said, "Fuck me, that's why you go to the butty shop so you can get out! Right, get your van in 32 and I will put them in", so I parked the van, walked to the security and said, "What do you fancy for breakfast, lads?" and they said, "We will get these; you always get them", and I said, "Don't worry. I pay on my company card." I took the order I got the order from the office staff and off I went, first to the butty shop, put in the order and paid then drove 400 metres away to this rat's unit and backed in. I took 4 ranges out of the van then said I would be back, and I drove to the butty shop, got the food, went back and gave all the food out. Then I drove the van into Bay 32 and gave Monk his butty and said, "Get 4 more in before you have that". I walked to security with the bag, I gave the boss and the office people theirs and walked into security. They had a brew ready for me. I got two butties out of the bag and said, "Fuck's sake! They have put them all in and left mine out, you bitch!" One of them said, "Have mine", and I said, "No, I will go back; it's only 5 minutes. I will get us a cake too", then went to my van. My butty was on the floor in the van, so I drove the van to the butty shop, got 5 cakes and dropped the cookers off. I went back to site, parked the van and walked in eating my butty and with a bag of cakes. On my way back, I rang Monk and said, "Meet me in security", so I walked in, had my butty and gave the cakes out and Monk just looked and shook his head. After we finished our food, Monk was walking out, and I shouted him and said, "Get another 4 into 32. I will be 5 to 8 minutes", so I went back with security and talked rugby, had a brew and a laugh and said, "Shit, I need some cable. Is there any electrical places or will I have to go to B&Q?" and they said, "No idea, mate". I said, "I will nip out in a bit. I will just drop my tools out of the van", so I was round to 32, backed in, opened doors - it took about 70 to 80 seconds to put 4 ranges in and I shut the doors and off I went. I stopped at security, asked if they needed anything then I drove out and did my drop, got paid and made my way back to site. I had the cable under the seat and I drove back in and when I drove past security, I lifted the cable and both arms like I had won the cup, but it was bluff tactic. So, I then drove and parked under 32, went into Monk and said, "Do you want to put another 4 in the van?" said he said, "Do you think we are pushing it?" and I said, "Monk, look around; there are hundreds of thousands of cookers. Do you think they will miss 12?" He said, "No, and I can write them off as damaged anyway and say they have been skipped", so I said, "Okay, bang 4 more in". He said, "You can't go out again", and I said, "No, I do this one on my way home", so he loaded me up then I went in and started my work list. When I was about to leave, I walked into Monk's office and asked him to come to the warehouse where there were no cameras. I said, "Here you go, mate", and gave him £8000 cash. He said, "Fuck me, what did you get, mate?" and I said, "I do them for £500 each as it's a quick drop and the cash is there." I was getting £600 per oven so after I left and did my drop on the way home, I had £9,600 in cash plus my wages for the day at around £800 plus VAT. It was like a dream job; you charged stupid money and you got anything you wanted from the site. Plus, now, I had 2 people willing to load the van for cash.

Now you can see the problem I had - to a normal person, you would think what a life, but I had started in a terraced house on £85 a week, doing my own work on a night to earn extra money. We wrote everything down in a little book so we knew what we had after the bills and the shopping and we would work out if we could afford to go out on a Saturday night with all the lads and their wives. We didn't miss many as I always made extra money somewhere in the week and the wife used to love going out with them all on a Saturday night. Even back then, I had to work weekends but we would get scrap iron or lead at weekends so I could go out on the Sunday night with all the lads. I loved that night; we had a riot every week, always doing something stupid. Now, I had hit a point that I couldn't go out as I did not want to risk getting pulled over on the Sunday morning and it was at weekends when I was making most of my money. In the 10 years, I had gone from £60k to £80k a year fiddling the insurance for people to earning £80k to £130k a month and the work was so easy it was unreal. With every job I did, if there was something else near my job that needed fixing, I would go and fix that and put it on my invoice, carry out repairs on this area as I had materials left over and there was no charge; they loved that - they thought I was amazing.

It ended up I had the total run of the place. My biggest problem was I was making too much through my company because I had no materials to claim back. It was just me paying managers for information on jobs and making 5 to 10 times what my original price was. I will give you an example: They wanted a new car park as the other was all cracked; all the topcoat had come away, so it needed to be taken out by a road planer machine and a new base then a new topcoat laid, and after that, all the white parking bays needed to be painted along with three zebra crossings. I was pricing the job along with a company who does the motorways so I thought, 'That's good for me', but I didn't know anyone who did this work and thought I may miss this one, but one of the lads gave me the number of an old guy who did Tarmac, so I got him out and it was a big car park, so he gave me a price of £30,000 - just the new road, no lines, and I said, "Listen, I know you're talking about wrapping up soon so what can you do for cash?" so, he said, "£22,000", so I said, "I will give you that if you can get someone to do the white lines". Then he said, "If you give me £23,000, I will get the lines sorted", and I said, "Don't forget to do those 3 little zebra crossings!" He called me a cheeky bastard and I said, "I know, mate, but it's business, plus, I will give you a nice case of wine!" I got hold of the boss I was dealing with and said, "Have you got the price in yet?" and he said, "Yes, meet me in the canteen at 9.30

am." When he got there, he said, "Listen, do you think you can do this as it is a big job?" and I said, "Come on, just give me the price." A big company had priced it and it was £128,350.00 plus another £4500,00 for all the road lines and zebra crossings, so I went home and altered what I had written to £125,500.00 and I put 'this includes all the road lines and zebra crossings' and the day after, I got confirmation asking me to send in my RAMS and a time scale so they could close off the car park. So, I said, "If you allow me to start on Friday, as everyone finishes at 12 noon and it is a Bank Holiday, I will try to get the tarmac down before the staff return". So, the boss rang me and said, "Mate, fucking no chance you will get that done. The other company said 2 weeks closed car park". I said, "Have faith, mate", then all the machinery came to site Friday first thing and we had started in some areas because there was space and as soon as the staff left, the planner drove with a wagon following catching the spelt off the conveyor and it was ready for base on Saturday and to my surprise, he had done the base by 1.30 pm. Then he said he had paid a little extra for Sunday delivery for top coat and fuck me, he was unreal! This man was 64 years old; he had 5 lads but the guy was like a machine! They had finished the car park, all cleaned and machines moved for Sunday 3 pm. I was impressed. On Monday, the line people came and Jo came to oversee the work they did, all the work on the estimate, plus some extra parking bays around the front of the main office. The total job looked brilliant. So, I called at his house with the cash and the wine and some flowers for his wife and I paid him £35,000. He said, "Why have you given me this?" and I said, "Because your work is brilliant. If you need anything off the site, just let me know and I will sort it, so, just give me your list and give me two days. I will drop off what you want at yours". He asked for a couple of things that were no problem, then on the Tuesday, when all the staff returned, they were made up with the work. We had the normal meeting and walked round and one of the directors said to me, "How the fuck do you do it? Every time you do a job, it is always done before the date you give and the place is spotless!" I said, "I had a street cleaner in yesterday to go over the site so it was tidy for when you got back", and he said, "Amazing! I have never known a builder like you!" and walked off. But I had also got in early on Bank Holiday Monday and put an envelope in my boss friend's drawer with £5000 inside. He was buzzing with it! He couldn't thank me enough and said, "Did you make enough to pay me this?" and I said, "Just about, pal".

Then we had another road job in Chester. I had to talk to one of the managers in private and I said, "What price have they come in with for Chester?" and he said, "Mate, it's not my job, but I will sort it tomorrow." I said, "I phoned the company who does the motorway white lines, and they want £880 plus VAT for each of the three zebra crossings", and he said, "I know, because I was listening to a conversation and he asked what I thought, and I said I know the white lines cost a lot as we had them done on the other site", so he had planted the seed for me. I was getting mine ready to send in and put the car park separate from the zebra crossings as they wanted new parking bays marked out and the charge was per parking bay. Then I did all my Risk and Method Statements. Just before I sent it, I got called into work and someone had vandalised the toilets. I went in about 4.30 pm and when I was getting all the water off the floor, the manager came in and he said, "Put this in your pocket, read it and burn it, please. I will only get the white line price tomorrow as a different company is doing it", so we looked at the toilets and I said, "I am going to re-pipe these and change the damaged toilet and the cracked sink". He said, "Don't do it all tonight. They are only expecting you to come in, clean up and make safe so the rest can be used", then he went home, so I fitted a new toilet and just fitted new piping on the feed pipes. I took the sink off, fitted two service valves on the hot and cold and blocked off the waste and it was about 8 pm, so I went to security and it was one of the young ones I had got some stuff for the week before. So, I went in and said, "Can you do me a favour? Will you sign me out at 11.45 pm, please? I am in tomorrow so I will sign the book", and he said, "Not a problem, pal". So, I went home and back the morning after, and he hadn't signed the out time, so I put 11.55 pm and back in at 7.30 am. All I had to do all day was fit this sink which I had fitted into position the night before with silicone, so I went for a walk round as I needed some bits out of a room. Then one of the managers said, "Are you going to the canteen for breakfast?" and I said, "Yes, what time?" He said, "9.15 am as it is empty", so I went off then met him in the canteen. I paid for me and him then we sat down. He said, "I need your estimate in today for the car park", and I said, "I will get it to you before 2 pm. I was that busy last night I did not have chance to read that price", and he said, "It is £108,600 for the car park, and £18,400 for the line men. If you can come back this morning with £98,400 for the car park and £15,000 for the lines and bays, you can do it". So, I said, "Right, let me get this sink done and I will send you my Estimate and RAMS." He said, "Put on yours that the cost includes any lines needed", so I got the sink done and I was back home for dinner. As instructed, I altered my estimate and sent it in for £984.00 Plus VAT, then I rang the manager and said, "Have a look; if you need it changing, send it back", and he said, "That's fine, mate. I can put it in now, but what about the lines?" and I told him it would be about £12,000, so 24 hours later, I got the confirmation of the job for the car park. I spoke to the guy who had done the last one for me and I said, "Cash again, mate", and he said, "Don't you ever give up?" I said, "No, and you're retiring soon!" He had a huge road planer on the back of a low loader, a very big JCB on another low loader and two wagons to take away the spoils. He got started and it was like watching them do the motorway. I asked if there was anything I could do, but he told me to go home and he would call me later. So, I left the site and called back later to see him. They had planed the full car park down ready for the base coat, so the planer was taken off-site with the big JCB then a Tarmac machine was brought in with a standard JCB and the Tarmac trucks fed the machine. They were brilliant, just following at the back of each other driving along tipping into the tarmac layer then changing over when he was empty. Then the huge road roller was driven over, then the topcoat was put down and rolled a few times. He had done it in 2 days, and it looked amazing. He said, "Just get these bays marked out", so they used a thin line of floor paint that the line men could tape up to, then the next day, the line men got the bays done so quickly, it was nice to watch. They did the three zebra crossings and then said, "Do you want us to repair the other two while we have the boiler running?" They went over the old ones, made them look new and I gave him £40. He said, "Cheers, pal. I will do the entrance near the main gate on the way out", and I said, "Thanks, mate. You have done a top job". So, with all the workmen off site, all the big bosses came out for a look, and one said, "How come we have had these others done?" and I said, "It's okay, it's in my price", so that got me big brownie points. They asked when it could be used. I said they could use it right away if they wanted and they said, "No, there is only a couple of hours. We will tell them Monday. Well done, mate, it looks great!" I paid the Tarmac man out of the £35,000 cash again; that was what I got paid off some stuff I had got from the other site, and I gave the manager £5000, left it in his drawer and then I had to get rid of the money I cleared that month. It was close to £300,000! I did a receipt from a Tarmac company for just over £89,000 plus VAT and moved that money to the China stock markets, then I put one in for the road lines and zebras. I made this look bigger as I added all the extra work to it and put it in for £39,600 plus VAT and moved that to the China stock markets. I also did a couple for around £20,000 each and put those cheques into my mate's bank so all the time I worked, I never took wages, but now you see why; it was coming at me from all angles. I used my mate's account as my float for paying people cash for doing their work.

A few weeks after that, I was back with Monk and we did a few runs over the next couple of months. He had got a taste for the money and he said, "There must be a quicker way of doing this". I said, "I can hire a 7.5-ton wagon if you want", and he said, "There is a new young lad on at the weekend; do you fancy it?" and I said, "Do you think he will be okay?" and Monk said, "I have already paid him for my mate to come in for something and I told him to be careful; the less sees, the less will know". So, the weekend came and I turned up in this 7.5-ton lorry. I got out and the lad said, "What are you doing in that?" and I said, "My fucking van broke down last night and my mate has a load of office furniture in the back he has to deliver Monday, so he said I could use it. I had no other option; it is a nightmare to drive".

I drove round the back and Monk had loads all ready to go in and he loaded it in around 8 minutes. I said, "How many is in there?" and he said, "30". I said, "Fuck me, pal", and I drove off out the site to my drop off. He unloaded me, then I drove back. I then got out and said to the security lad, "I am going for some butties in a bit.

What do you fancy?" He asked how much but I said I would get it so I went round the back, loaded again and then back off site, stopped at the butty shop, put the order in and did my drop. Rat boy, the drop man, asked if we could do a deal since there were so many but I said he could load them back up, so he handed over £36,000 in cash and said, "Are you coming back?" I told him to fuck off then picked the butties up and went back. I gave security lad his and he thought I was amazing. Then I went into the toilet to work out my funds. After that, I went to Monk and said to him, "What a cheeky twat he is! He wanted a deal because there were so many and I said I would have to see you. He wants them for £400 so I have not taken any money off him until I had spoken to you. The only good thing is it is an easy drop, mate; it is 4 minutes away and he has to de-badge them and sell as damaged repaired", and Monk said, "Right, I didn't know that". I said, "He can't sell them when the serial number on, so he sells as repaired, but he still gets £700 to £800 for each one." Monk said, "Do it, mate; let him have them for £400 as there is 60, so that's a lot to take".

So, I gave Monk a list and said, "Can you put these in for me and lend me your car while I go and sort that deal out?" I went out in his car and just had a drive round for a bit then drove back to site and stopped at the toilet with my big green coat on and put £12,000 in an envelope, walked round the site and to the wagon.

No one was there so I put £24,000 under the driver's seat and went into Monk's office and said, "Here you go, pal, £12,000 in cash". He said, "Mate, that is close to 6 months' wages. I have not been to the bank since I met you!" and we both had a laugh in his office. I said, "I am not doing these lights now", and he said, "Can you do the ones in the fork truck bay as they can't see anything?" So, I said, "Yes, mate, I will do them now and I won't come to you again. Save anybody talking about us both getting on!" I walked down to the fuse board for the area and turned back on the fork truck bay and 2 sets of fuses that do the lights outside on the yard. All of these were on my list but all I had done on Wednesday to get back at the weekend was turn some of the fuses off. It was something I had been doing for some time as no one would go near the fuse board, but sometimes I had to take the full front off and put a barrier round me, so it looked like something had gone wrong inside, then I would go home and charge for supply and fit of new tube/bulbs in the warehouse lights or outside on the yard. Then I would just turn on the fuse and get paid for fixing the lights. My Saturday also came with a bill for £950 plus VAT; it was that price as the bloke I paid could only authorise up to £1000.

The following week, I was back at the Manchester site where they made the products, and I was asked to price a new showroom, 30 metres square, in 6-inch solid blocks with the inside dry-lined and plastered, with a new door cut into the wall and two double oak doors at each end to get the products in. So, after doing a drawing and getting it passed, I had to get prices for the blocks and plastering and the doors and electrics, so when I got home from the gym, I sat on my computer and started to get everything priced up. I got the bricklayers sorted and then I got all the prices in and it was around £38,000 plus VAT. Next day on site, I was doing all my repair stuff and one of the managers came over and I said, "You okay, pal?" and he said great, and I said, "We came in at 7.15 am and I put a drink in your drawer", and he said, "You didn't have to, mate". I told him it was because I had been told I was pricing with someone else for the showroom and he said, "Listen, anything over £5000 and we have to have 2 estimates". He asked how far I had got and I said I was just waiting for the 3 brickies to get back with a price as they charge per block. He said, "Right, I should have the other back tomorrow. The next day on site, he came over and said, "I have got the other one back in", and he gave me a piece of paper. He said, "The full breakdown is on that and the price but no other information, so burn it when you have looked and don't word yours in the same way". I told him I would sort it later, then we got on with our work and I didn't get chance to see him again, so we left about 2.30 pm and got home for 3.30 pm and I sat at my computer and looked at the estimate he had given me. It didn't have the company name on, just the wording and the price. They made it sound as though they were building a hotel! The page was just full of posh shite to make the job look ten times bigger, but they were also fitting a plank vinyl floor in oak to match the doors, but it was costing £128,000 plus VAT. So, I phoned the manager and said, "This is high this, mate," and he said, "Why? What have you got yours to?" and I said, "I am near £80,000 but I have not priced the floor". He said, "Did they ask you?" and I said, "No, I wasn't told", so he said, "Get a price for the floor and leave it out; don't mention the floor in your estimate". So, I went in at £109,900 plus VAT and sent it to him. He told me to expect a call this afternoon on the floor. I couldn't ask him any questions on his email because they could be opened by the site IT Department if they suspected anything, so around 3.30 pm, one of the head managers rang. He was okay but wouldn't take a bung, so I just played it cool with him. He asked me to price laying a floor inside on completion, so I acted daft and asked what type of laminate, or would they want vinyl and he said they liked the Karndean. I said, "I bet they do! That is the dearest floor they do. I had my summer house done and it cost me £2100 and mine is only 8 metres x 4 metres. This one is 30 metres square, so I will ring my flooring man who did your office and get a price and get back to you." He asked if I could get back to him before 5 pm as there was a meeting so I said I would try my best. I rang my floor man and told him the details and asked for a rough estimate and he told me the rough cost per metre supplied and fitted. I just put a bit onto it, and I put the price in at £12,000 supplied and fitted and sent it in, so I ended up with this job, and again, the brickies did all the work! It took them 3 days as it was only 3 walls since it was being joined to another building, so that then became a saving of 30 metres by 14 courses high on the blocks. Over the next few days, the bricks went off, we fitted the door frames, started to dry-line then I jumped on the plastering, so we were all done and the room clean for Thursday. The floor layer came in on Saturday and I went in front screeding the glue out and he followed me laying the planks. We stayed and finished just after 5.30 pm the same night and that was me done. It took me, in total, 9 days. I paid the bricklayers £2400; the materials came to just over £12,000 including both of the doors, and all the electric stuff I got free of charge, and the floor layer was £4800 because we used cheaper flooring. So, after paying the plasterer and a few bits and giving the security men a drink, I had spent around £22,000 and my price was £121.900 plus £3000 for extra work that was done after each site visit; he always wanted something else added like extra sockets, then 16 data points, so it ended up at £124,900 plus VAT. Then I had to get on my computer and re-do all the invoices I had received and I had to change the bill to £68,600 plus VAT and give my mate the cheque. I changed the floor bill and took it up to £34,800 plus VAT to supply and fit 40 metres square with the full room screeded first, then laid in the Karndean. I also added all the door strips in too, so it all looked like that price was real and again, gave my mate the cheque and just put the floor company on the cheque stub for my accountant who I think was starting to ask questions by now. I even had 4 different types of paper, so the invoices looked different even though they were written in a different font, but I did have the best accountant in Manchester; he was amazing.

I would go out the odd time with my cousin's friends; they were about 10 years younger than me, but a great set of lads. About 15 to 20 used to go out together; they had gone to school together then had stayed friends growing up. Every time I went out, I always took around £500 and I would buy loads of the drinks through the night. We used to have a great laugh. One night, one of the lads who used to be the life and soul of a party was just sat on his own and I could see there was something wrong with him. I took a couple of drinks over and a couple of brandies and sat with him and said, "What's up, pal? You have been quiet as fuck all night." He said, "To be truthful, if you hadn't been buying the drinks, I would have gone home hours ago. I am broke, I have no money and I have missed two months on my mortgage". I said, "Fuck me, why didn't you ring and why haven't all these lot helped you out?" and he said, "These are good friends but they wouldn't do that for you". So, I gave him £50 and said, "Right, that's to have a good night tomorrow. Come to mine after I finish work". He asked if I was sure and I said, "Get to the bar - your round". He got a couple of drinks and gave me a huge hug. When he came round, we sat down and I said, "What do you owe on your home?" and he said, "£920 then this month's", so I went away and came back and gave him £2000 and said, "Right, pay your house then you have some extra for any other bills". Then he cried a little. I said, "Mate, that is what we are here for!" He said, "I start my new job next week and the wife has got a part-time, so I will get the money back to you." I said not to rush. So, I hadn't seen them for a couple of months as I was busy at work and not going out. It was the second week in December and I was doing my work on the computer and there was a knock on the door. The wife answered and said, "Come in, he is in the office". So, he walks in and I said, "How are you, pal?" and he said, "I am loads better, mate, and I wanted to bring you this since it is getting close to Christmas. There is only £1450 here but I will sort the rest. I just wanted to make sure you had some money for Christmas." Then I stood up and said, "Mate, thank you so much. You have been very true to your word". I put the envelope back into his coat pocket and he said, "What are you doing?" and I said, "Please, it is Christmas; you need it more than me, so keep it. Call the bill quits and you enjoy your Christmas with the extra money you have saved". He said, "Are you sure, mate? I feel bad", and I said, "Don't feel bad, just have a good

Christmas with the wife and kids!" He hugged me and cried and said, "No one has ever helped me before", and I said, "If you need help, just ask; don't suffer in silence". After he went, it made me feel good.

I also got on very well with the girls at the companies that I worked for because I used to look after them. If they were going out, I would put £400 in a card and say 'have a drink on me' or if anyone who used to do the payments to my company was getting married, I would put £1000 in a card for their wedding so it didn't matter what I wanted or needed, everyone gave it to me.

By this time, I had no idea how much money I had, so I asked for a statement to be sent to me with my totals on, just for me to see how far I was from my target. Anyway, it came, and I had hit the £2 million months before, and if you added in my home, it was 2.5 million and I had money in 12 different bank accounts. One bank had £670,000 in it! It was crazy, so I ended up giving my kids enough money to buy their homes. I had paid for their university and the homes they stayed in, plus paid them £85 a week wages for them to live on as I didn't want them to come out with a big bill. I also paid for their driving lessons, bought both of them their first two cars and I paid the insurance. I also paid for my in-laws' holidays for 5 years - the last one cost £27,900 – plus, I gave them spending money. I paid for their car and my wife's car and she also had a company card to put fuel in and I paid the insurance on the cars and the home. All she paid was food but I used to give her £200 at the end of the month because she had run out of money. She had a good job; she was a top manager and getting £46,000 a year but I still paid for everything. Not once since I met her did she bring her purse out with her; she just wanted the best of the best, so I ended up giving both kids some more money, another £50,000 each and I gave her brother £25,000 as I wanted to get rid of the money now because I had made it and it didn't bother me. If I went out at the weekend with the lads, I would take £500 and blow it on my mates. I wanted people to have a good time and I would sooner give my girls some now I am in my 40s so they don't have to struggle like I did all my life. They could be debt-free and mortgage-free too as I always told them you need to get rid of your mortgage as soon as you can. I used to give £1000 to people who were struggling at Christmas and each Christmas, I would help 2 or 3 people and they loved me and I was proud of what I was doing. I used to sponsor the local rugby team, the local football, the girls' football and the girls' dance centre and it got my company name on everything, but I didn't do it for that; I did it because I just wanted to help and people respected me for doing it.

I did this for around 12 years and my wife used to hate me doing it because she would call them scruffs, but I came from a council estate and I know what some people go through to bring up children; even more so if they are single parents. I did a lot of sponsors for kids from rugby football to dancing and I was helping people to do what they loved but couldn't afford. When I was young, I was that lad with no kit, no boots and no bag. It's not nice looking at everyone in the changing room with a bag. Even daft things like soap, shampoo and a towel - I had none of that. I got showered in cold water and had to dry myself on the top I had just done PE in, so you were looked down on. That's why I helped them. I also did it for self-satisfaction. I loved it when people would hug me, and listening to people talking about you, it was a big morale boost. I know no one helped me but I am not like these other people - you should never look down on anyone because you never know what's round the corner.

It was strange; I had all this money and didn't spend any of it on myself. As I got older, I put on a few pounds and thought, 'Right, I have 12 pairs of jeans that won't fit me, so what can I do?' So, I opened an account with a local men's clothing shop in the town centre, Burtons, and you could order online. First of all, I went into the shop and bought two pairs of jeans that fitted me as I was now a 34 waist. I took them home, took the labels off and put them onto two pairs of my 32-waist jeans and took them back the day after. The girl said, "Are they okay?" and I said, "Great, just a little tight, that's all", so she gave me two more pair of 34-waist jeans and didn't change the receipt. I went back on the Monday but the same girl was on, so I left it until later and went back again when it was a young lad. I took two more pairs of my old 32 waists back and went through the story but he refunded my money, so I thought, 'Great, 4 down, 8 to go'. I gave it a week and went to a store in the next town, and it was just the same, so I swapped 4 pairs in that shop and I gave it a few weeks then went back to my local one and swapped the others, so I had swapped 12 pairs of 32-waist jeans for 12 new pairs of 34 waist. The only problem was some of my old ones were a couple of years old but I didn't care. Most things were online, and the shop sold designer stuff like Hugo Boss and all the others online. I had about 6 T-shirts that my mate had got me from Turkey. They were shite! I was a large and these were as tight as hell, so I ordered 2 Boss T-shirts and they let you know when they were in and they were £120 for one and £95 for the other so I got them home and I had ordered XL as they are a small fit. I had to cut into the label to get the tags out without damaging them then I put a small hole in the fake ones and fed the tags back through one of them. I had to super glue the back so I waited until a Saturday as I knew it would be busy and I took them back just before 1 pm as staff go on their dinner break at that time. There was a couple waiting at the counter then it was me, so I went up and said to the young girl, "Why is such a stunning girl like you working in here? You should be modelling", and she blushed and said, "Thank you!" I kept her talking so she just took them out of the bag; they were sealed in the plastic bag with the barcode showing. She asked if anything was wrong with them and I said, "I would have kept them if you had been inside, but they are a little tight", so she just refunded my money. I ended up going through my wardrobe. I even did a couple for my mate who was panicking to take his fake ones back, so I took them for him; it was like a game.

I never ever had problems getting lads to work for me with one day's notice because I paid good money so they could not refuse. I did have one lad who was good to work with and he did a couple of years for me but the more money I gave him, the more money he would lend; it was crazy. Then I found out why - he was hitting the booze and cocaine. One weekend, I had to put some stuff in his garage. There was about £8000 worth and the week after, I said, "I am coming to yours for that stuff", and he said, "Mate, I have had my garage broken into". I let it go and about six months later, I was at a rugby match and one of the big drug dealers was there and shouted me so I went over. He started chatting about work and he wanted something. I said, "It will be at yours on Monday night". He gave me a big bag of cocaine and I said, "Mate, I don't use it. Thanks for the offer". Then he said, "You can pay your mate at work with it", and I said, "No, he gets paid well but does lend money!" He then said, "A few months ago, he owed me £5000 and I went to his house and took everything out of his house and a load of stuff out of his garage". I said, "You want fucking; that was my stuff" and he said, "Sorry, Tuck. I will sort it. How much do I owe you?" and I said,

"No, leave it if it has cleared his bill off". We shook hands and I dropped off a gift for him on Monday night. Then I went back to work the day after and said to my labourer, "When you got your garage broken into, did they take anything else?" and he said, "No". I said, "Did you owe anyone any money at the time?" and he said, "No", so I said, "Come on". He got in the van and I took him home and he said, "Same time tomorrow?" and I said, "No, mate. You're not coming back. I spoke to Dez and he told me about your garage and you know I hate people who lie so I know now I can't trust you anymore; sorry". He said, "Tuck, please, I would never take anything from you", and I said, "You did, mate; £8000 worth of items in your garage to pay your bill. Goodbye".

By this time, I had got my money well down and I didn't care. I wanted both my kids to be mortgage-free just like me and I wanted them to have extra in the stock market to fall back on. My wife used to go mad; "Why are you giving them money again?" and I said, "I would sooner give it to them now when they need it than let them struggle through life and me give it to them when I die. This way, they will have less stress." Even though she had never contributed to the savings at any point in her life, she had plenty to say when I was giving it away. She always said to me, "If we ever split, I would never come for your money", and, like an idiot, I believed her. I had got my savings down to around £800,000 and thought, 'That's enough for when we finish'. I had no thoughts of wrapping my job up because I loved what I was doing and I was getting very good money, so I bought a few watches as I didn't have one and ended up with around 24 Rolex, Tag and Patek Philip. I had bought a Rolex for my wife and her mum, her dad got a Tag and I got my girls and their partners Cartier watches. I think that one Christmas cost me the £3000 I used to give the wife to buy all the gifts plus around £35,000 on watches as an after-dinner surprise gift, but I loved every minute of it because they were all made up with their watches. I took my wife to meet my friend who deals in watches and diamonds and ended up getting her a platinum ring with a £5500 diamond in the middle, but she was very ungrateful. Even when I got her the best car and paid for the car insurance and her fuel, she didn't give a fuck about me; as long as I will still earning money, she wasn't bothered.

My relationship with Monk was very strong and I had to keep it that way as he was loading my van through the week and I was taking over £6000 cash per week through him. Then one of my best friends finished work and I was watching rugby and he was there watching his son. We had knocked about together since we were in the infant school and we used to do a lot of stuff together when he was warehouse manager at the big food store. We got on great - he was one of the best friends you could ever have; he was always there for you. We started going and getting sorted through Monk and I thought it would be nice to give him a couple of thousand, so I said to him, "We will go into work tomorrow at 4 am, and, as there is no night shift and I have a Merc Sprinter long wheelbase, if we put the cookers on their side, we could load ten in the back". We only did this if the right security man was on nights, and he would say, "Fuck me, why are you here so early?" and I would say, "Oh, I have got a hospital appointment". We would drive the van to the side door, run round with a sack truck getting them to the door, then we would carry them out and put them in the van. Good stacking got you 10 fitted tight, then we would park up and do the work that was on the sheet. Then, 30 minutes before break, I would get the butty order and go out, order the food and unload the van, get paid and pick the food up on the way back. I would have my food with the lads so I could give my mate £2000, and I would end up with £4600. Don't get me wrong; it was very hard work, but it was worth it. Plus, when we got back, we had an empty van so could get whatever was on my list for my friends and people who use to look after me with stuff for work.

We had to go to the Blackburn site one day and when we got there it was fully loaded with every small appliance that you plugged in around the kitchen. I said to my mate, "Right, list what you want for you, your kids and family and I will do the same. Anything extra we will give to the lads who sort me with materials and the skip company". So, as well as getting paid over £680 plus VAT for the day, you were getting everything you needed, so, when we got home, we spent 2 hours dropping stuff off for other people, so we were pleasing everyone. We ended up going back to Monk's site but didn't have any plans for anything that day as we wanted to get off handy, but when I walked in, the security man said, "Can you go and see the boss before you start?" The boss, who was a director, was a huge fan of mine. He loved what I did and always made sure I had plenty of work. So, when I got to his office, he said, "Sit down, mate". I was a little bit in panic mode and was thinking of excuses for anything he had to say, but he started off by saying, "Thanks for coming in. I need your help. We have had a lot of items go missing." I said, "I always ask if I need anything", and he said, "I know, and you're always welcome, you know that, but have you seen anything as you are all over the site?" Then I said, "I have seen some of the fork truck drivers leave pallets of brass fittings at the back of the yard and I know this as Monk had told me". said he asked, "Did you see who it was?" and I said, "No, but they are still there". Then he said, "It's okay, the camera is facing the pallet", and I thought, 'Thank fuck! I was going to take them this week'! He then said, "We are getting trailers back with extra products on it. One trailer had 12 large range cookers". I said, "Thinking back a few weeks, a driver told security what bay his load was on and they said no, it had been changed. They said he was to take this trailer off one of the trailer parks to another company. Anyway, he lost his shit and I thought that's strange. But now, thinking about it, the lad on later loads his trailer as you know where they are going the day before and he tells him what bay it is loaded under so he can relay that information to security. Then he gets the paperwork, gets the trailer and takes off what's extra, then drops the rest of the delivery, but when he is given another trailer, like when he lost his shit that day, another driver is allocated that trailer that's loaded with the extras, and because there are extras on the trailer, that's why you are getting returns". He said, "You're a smart man, but how do we nail him?" I said, "Look at the list of all the returned items, then you can eliminate each driver who has returned the extras on each trailer and that will only leave you with a couple to watch." He was really pleased and said, "At least now we have a place to start". So, I said, "Speaking of starting, boss, can I get started? I have lost over an hour with you and I have a hospital appointment later." He said, "No matter how much you do, just send the work list to me and I will make sure you don't lose anything".

When I got back, I told my mate all about it and he said, "Fuck, it's a good job we left it this morning", and I said, "We will leave it a couple of weeks now". I went in to see Monk and told him and he said he knew about it and there was a meeting later, so I said, "Just leave it for a bit now, pal". We got back to our work and we had it done in less than 2 hours, so we left at dinner time. I had a job to price that afternoon, so I needed to get back but at least we'd had good warning so we had a coffee and a chat and decided to pull taking anything from the site.

When we got back to the Manchester site, I had loads of friends there and I was paying every manager that could do me some type of service. One of the best was the fork truck driver preparing damaged concrete on the yard as this paid top money. It was even better when they asked me to price up a trailer park on site, so I said, "What about all the spoils that come off; do you want it off site or spread round the site?" They told me to get shot of it, so I had wagons coming in, getting filled up and leaving a 16-ton roll off for surplice, so we got the 6 parking bays dug out, all the hardcore fitted and plated down, then we shuttered each one out and on the first day, we poured numbers 1, 3 and 6, then later that day, took the forms out and set up to do the infill ones the day after. I have to say the job looked awesome. I had even run a 3-inch pipe from the light on the post to the centre of the concrete at the back and then I fitted a lamp post we had spare and I fitted two 250 LED lights on the lamps and consented into the small light sign on the edge of the road. We had got everything finished around 4.40 pm and then the lights came on, followed by the two new lights at the back and it looked amazing, so I walked in to get the big boss and the guy who had drawn it out. When they both came out, the main boss said, "So was there lights at the back?" and I said, "No, but I had a spare lamp stand, Armco cable and some LED lights and we already had a light fitting bracket and it was just easy to join into the signpost and even down to the timer". The main big boss was just stumped. He said, "It looks great, mate, and the place is spotless", and I said, "I like to keep it all clean". He then got his paperwork out and said, "You know what, you haven't priced for fitting the lamp and lights". I said, "It's okay, have it on me then, but HSE will make you fit one anyway. That's why I did it or we would have to cut the concrete up to get the cable in, so it's better to do it now". He said that was great and to send in an invoice, which I did as soon as I got home. When I went in a couple of days later, I was called in to a meeting and I had no idea what was going on, but they were talking about the light and how pleased they were for me supplying and fitting. Someone said, "You can't expect the builder to pay for a lamp stand and install lights at the back free of charge. He does more than enough for us for free". So, they had priced the lamp, the cable and the lights that I had got free off one of my mates and they came back with an offer of £800 plus VAT for doing it. I said, "It's not all about the money. I love working here and I knew it needed lights at the back, so I just thought if I just do the job, it doesn't look like I am asking for extra money". Then the boss said, "Mate, we like what you do, and we understand you have our best interest in mind at all times. Thank you for offering us this and I just want to know if £800 plus VAT is enough for what you have done". So, I told him, "If you want to pay that then yes, it is fine". It was one of the managers I paid who was doing my invoice and he said, "Mate, we have your first price of £64,000, then you were asked to dig another bay out at the side, so I have put that down as £13,995 and I have put this with your £64k and took it to £79,500. If you're happy with that, do me the invoice and put the VAT on and I will get it in for next week's BACS run." I worked it out and it was just under £100,000 and it took us 4 days to complete. I usually paid the lads £80 per day and £100 for weekends, so I gave all four of them £600 and it was worth every penny.

Everything we dug out was tipped on site to build some ground up and the concrete cost me just over £12,000 as I gave the driver £100 each day, so once again, I needed to get rid of 90% of that money through invoices from other companies and giving my mate the cheque to put in his account. I left £12,000 in the job as I had invoices to clear it, so I got the relief and the VAT back on the materials. This was the only way of moving money away from your account and then he would put it in the stock market for me and keep a few hundred for himself. I had a great system and it worked for everyone.

I was the looking at a post someone in my family had put on Facebook and I had noticed that a guy with the same name as the Big Beast when I was a kid had replied and when I checked my sister's profile, he was her friend. So, I went onto his profile but there was a lack of information about where he lived, so later

On, I had to meet up with a lad who had asked me to do a run for him (a run was dropping something off far away). Anyway, the run kept getting pushed back and he had asked because I was going to Blackburn so I said, "How much would you charge me to get shot of a guy?" and he said, "For you, nothing. Have you got his full information, address and picture and the time he is home from work?" I said, "No, but I will get it." He said, "Does he owe you money?" and I said, "No, it's worse". The run didn't end up coming off, but they were paying anywhere between £10,000 and £50,000, depending on what was moving. All I was going to do was send one of my lads on the run, then send him to site to collect some light fittings for the other site, then come home, but the harder I looked, the harder The Beast was to find. Also, I wanted to be there when it was done, and the lad said that that could not happen as it was high risk and these people go alone so I was still thinking of doing it myself. It put me in a huge downer thinking about it and what to do, so when I finished, I went my mates and then went home, but after I had a shower, I was sitting at the bottom of the stairs with my iPad, but all I was doing was running my shit childhood through my head. I thought about each time I had been in his house.

Why was I still thinking about it after all this time? I had enough going on at work as I was sat typing most nights until midnight and past just to get the estimates altered so I could pay everyone who worked there. I even hit a point where I ran out of cash and one of my mates said, "I have a £3000 cash job in. Do you want to give me a cheque for £3600 and I will give you the £3000 cash?" I had to do it as my accountant said, "Try not to take any cash for a couple of weeks". It was my own fault as all the money I was getting off the stock, I was giving my mate to put in his company account, then moving it over into my stock market account for me. I should have kept hold of some but my head was up my arse. I had to do it this time as I needed money for the Monday, and by Friday, the full £3000 had gone to managers, staff, security and wages.

I was then asked to build another showroom, but this time, on the Manchester site as they wanted to use the old showroom as a display area for the new products, so again, I said to my mate, "Do I need to write this or can you get it to me?" He said, "I know the budget is £150,000 and it is not as complicated as the last one, so I would put your price at £122,000 plus VAT. I had set my price at £92,500 plus VAT, but when I rang him, he said, "Hello! How are you? Yes, no problem, just the normal please, pal; that will be fine", so I changed mine to £122,000 plus VAT and sent it in. They wanted one double oak door and one door leading into the room from the display room, so I rang the manager and said, "There is already a door leading into that new room", and he said, "Great! Next Tuesday, we are calling down, so see if you can get the beads on by then". for the brickies I had lined up were done by Saturday and just 2 were coming back on Sunday to finish some bits and point up, then I got the factory road cleaner, took all the big bits out and then cleaned the floors a few times just leaving it to be mopped. I took the beads off the door that was already in and filled the sides with foam and then we started to clean that big display room. We got it all hoovered to and the boss came with the manager and looked round. He said to me, "How the fuck do you organise and complete these in such a short time frame and do such a good job?" and I said, "Do you want me to be truthful?" and he said, "Yes", so, I said, "You have to flood it with men; like, get 6 bricklayers and 3 brickies' labourers, then put on 3 floating labourers. These will keep everything ready to bring in and keep everywhere cleaned up. We also buy ready-mixed mortar; it costs a little more, but saves 2 men mixing all day. It just means me bringing it on the fork truck, same as the blocks, lifting them up and driving along the scaffolding, stopping so they can load the boards up while the brickie is out of the way. As soon as that's done, pick up the tub of ready-mixed mortar and lift that up so they can use the spade to load all the boards up and then leave a tub at the middle of each wall for them to feed the brickies with. Meanwhile, the floating labourers can carry on cleaning round inside and out and make sure the site is clean so we don't have to do it at the end". He then said to me, "I will tell you what, mate, you know how to run a job!" and I said, "Thank you, but I have been doing this a long time and I want my work to be perfect because everyone that comes in here will know that I have done the building work and I like to keep a good name for my company". He said, "Well, it's working, pal", and off they went back to Blackburn.

I did have to write some big cheques to get rid of some money out of my company.

I know I put two cheques in two accounts, one for £48,680.00 and the other one went into the bank next door for £36,400.00 but I was still showing over £120,000.00 in my company account, so I spoke to my accountant and I ended up buying a new van and doing some more receipts for heavy plant machinery. I got it down to £26,000 and before my VAT, I took out a £10,000 dividend. My accountant said,

"You're pushing it, mate", and I said, "I know, but I am not working 12-hour days, 7 days a week and paying it all over to the VAT and tax. That's not right." He said, "You need to pay some VAT, mate", and I said, "Fine, but keep it round £3000". He said, "What will you do if you get inspected?" and I said, "I will go right to the closest mental hospital and sign myself in! I have been on antidepressants for 12 years and this is the reason I had no idea what I was doing. That's what you will say too; just say you kept asking me for paperwork and I was bringing all sorts of wrong stuff in, so my first line of defence is to act as stupid as you can and if it means going into the mental hospital for a month, the rest will do me good."

So now back with Monk, and my old rugby team was having a summer fun day to raise money for the club and one of my close friends said, "Have you got anything at home you can throw in, pal, small electrical stuff?" so I said, "Leave it with me". I spoke to Monk and he said, "What stuff do you want, mate, cookers? Hobs?" and I said, "No, small stuff - a couple of kettles and toasters and if have any hoovers as it is to raffle off. I normally buy stuff and give it to them as I played there for over 9 years and still have good friends who are coaches and managers". So Monk said, "Put your van under the normal place and I will get you a mixture". I left him and went into a meeting and then got my work done. It was about 3.30 pm but we used to leave around 2 pm and the manager, who I had just paid £200, said to me, "You're up to something, you cunt!" and I said, "I don't know what you mean. I have asked if any Hoover, Neff or Smeg small appliances have come in on returns", and he said, "Why, what you after?" When I told him, he said, "Why didn't you ask before?" and I said, "I don't like to keep asking you", so I gave my mate the van key and told him to lock the van and leave it where it was. Next thing, the manager came over with 4 big brown boxes and he said, "There is a mixture for you, mate".

There was a box of kettles, a box of toasters, a box of blenders and a box of smoothie makers and there were 4 in each box. I said, "Mate, that is so good of you. I will get done and bring the van round." I didn't know what Monk had put in, so I was hoping he wouldn't come to the van. We talked for a bit then someone came out and shouted him and he said, "Have you got your master key for the fork trucks?" and I said yes so, he said, "Move these boxes and do me a favour and put the truck back in the bay", and I said,

"No problem, mate. You get to your phone call". I drove to the van, put the stuff in and then parked the truck up and left the site without telling anyone.

When I got home, I looked in the back and Monk had put a sheet over the stuff he had put in. I had 2 boxes of kettles, 4 hoovers, 4 toasters, 4 bread makers, 8 boxes of pans, a box of food blenders, 4 slow cookers, 8 irons and 6 electric knives, so I put them all in my garage and asked the wife what she wanted out of the stuff for her friends at work. I sorted my in-laws and my mates out then took boxed stuff to the club - 2 kettles, 2 matching 4-slice toasters, 2 bread makers 2 electric knives, 2 irons, 1 blender and 1 slow cooker and they put them all in the raffle and made good money for the club.

The only things I kept were 1 iron, 1 kettle, 1 toaster, 1 soup maker and 1 slow cooker. I gave everything else away for free. I even ended up giving away all the stuff we had kept so I ended up with fuck all, but I didn't mind and when I went back up, I took a card signed by all the lads to say thanks to the manager. I just put on it 'thank you for your help and signed shirt donation to the club' and gave him a tray of Red Bull as he loved it. When he saw it, he said to me, "What fucking shirt?" and I had to explain to him that it was so people didn't ask what he had donated. He asked me to come to the canteen for a coffee and while we were there, he said, "I have got some stuff I need you to get rid of. Same as last time, we are clearing the old stock and there are about 4 pallets of brass", so I said, "Mate, that's great but because you give your work credit card in for your payment, I had to pay tax on the last lot of money", (that was bullshit) so he said, "That's fine; take your tax out of it and we will split it then. Go and see Monk as he knows what's going; there is 4 pallets", so I finished the coffee and then said, "What do I do about the list you have sent me? I won't get it done if I am taking this stuff". He said, "Don't worry; just send me a bill for £950 plus VAT for some concrete repairs". So, I went to see Monk and while I was with him, I gave him the same shit story about paying tax because it was going through my company and he was fine with it. Then he said, "There's actually 11 pallets. I told the manager there were only 4 so the first lot is ours". So, we put 7 pallets in and took them away and I cleared just over £87,820 in my old company account. When I went back, I told Monk we had got just under £40,000, so he said, "I worked it out; you take £10,000 for your tax and we get £15,000 each", so we then put the other 4 pallets on. Because they were very heavy, which Monk wouldn't have known because he used the for truck to load them, they came to just over £53,400, so I went back and told him that this load had only paid £19,850.

So, he sat down and said, "You take £5000 for your tax and we will split with the manager and give him £5000." So, I said, "Great, I will bring the cash in next week, mate". When I got home and worked it out, I had cleared close to £120,000 in one day plus the £950 plus VAT for doing nothing, so I got the money out of my safe and after the following week, I took in £18,500 for Monk and £5000 for the manger. Monk said, "Here, mate", and gave me a thousand pounds back. He said, "I will give him £4000 because he doesn't know", and I said, "Are you sure, mate?" and he said, "Yes. I need you to come over after; I need a chat", so I said okay and started on my jobs.

I was thinking about it most the morning, 'I bet he had spoken to the scrap place and he knows how much I got', so I was panicking all morning and then I went to see him. He said, "I didn't tell you last week, but I am getting a divorce. I need money to put down on a place". I said, "Fuck me, Monk, you have had thousands", and he said, "I know, and it's all saved. Can you come in this weekend with that big wagon off your mate?" I said, "I will try but I will have to see if Rat Boy wants them", so I rang him, and he said he had been ripped off by a bloke who used to buy off him. He took 12 cookers and didn't pay him, so I said, "Do you need more stock?" and he said, "I will but I can only pay you in two weeks". So I asked, "What's the guarantee you're going to pay me?" and he said, "Fuck me, Tuck, you're the last person I wouldn't pay! You would fucking kill me!" and I said, "You're right there, mate, I would, but I will see you Saturday around 7 am". I went back to Monk and said, "He doesn't want any, mate", and Monk was panicking then. So I thought, 'Monk needs the money', so I said, "Right, I will sort it, but to get back to site, I will have to switch a couple fuses off in the fuse board and then you can get the security to call me out on the Saturday and I will sort transport." So, Monk was happy and I said, "Get them to ring me at 7 am and I will see you on site". I went home and organised a 7.5-ton wagon to collect on Friday night because I knew what was going to happen. Either I would turn up on Saturday and tell Monk I got him to agree to £450 or Monk would ring and say, "Mate, ring him and tell him you will do £400 per unit". So, I waited and nothing, then the next day, I was on the site in Old

Swan Liverpool and my phone rang. It was Monk, and he said, "Mate, just go for the £400 he offered, and the lights are still out. and I will get security to call you on Saturday morning". I told him, "I have looked who is on security and it is our friend. Tell him on Friday those bays are not working, and tell him to ring me the same day. On Friday night, I got the wagon and took it to Blackburn, went into security and had a brew with him and said, "Did Monk tell you I was dropping some stuff for him?" and he said, "Yes, mate", so I drove round and Monk put 30 in the back. I took to the lad's unit and unloaded, then went back and put another 30 on and dropped them. After that, I picked the butties up and went into security and took him the big butty; he was made up. I drove round to Monk and got out of the wagon and said, "I have got us some food", and we sat in his office. He said, "Ring your mate and see if he will take another load", and I said, "Are you sure, mate? That's a lot of stuff!" and he said, "Fuck it, I am leaving next week!" I asked him, "What the fuck will I do then?" and he said, "Well, if I was you, I wouldn't take anything for at least a month as next week is stocktake and with all the stuff that's missing, the shit will hit the fan. So today, I will be going home in an ambulance; that's why I didn't come in my car. I suffer with anxiety and it feels like a heart attack, so I know what to do". So, I said, "Then that gets you out of the firing line because you're off sick?" and he said yes so, I told him to load it up because if Rat Boy didn't want them, I had another place they could have gone, so I rang him and said, "Don't lock up as I am coming back with a couple more", so Monk loaded the wagon and I took it to his unit. When I backed in and opened up, he said, "Fuck me, I can't take all of them, mate", and I said, "The bloke who gets them is going off sick so this is it for a good few months", so he said ok, and we got unloaded and I said, "How much have you got on you and in your safe?" and he said, "I only have £20,000", so I said, "Give me that and I will call on Wednesday to get the rest", so I took £4000 out of the money and went back and said to Monk, "Listen, he has only got £16,000 in his safe so I said I would call at the end of next week to get the other £20,000." Monk swore and I said, "Hang on, we have just pushed another 30 units on him that he didn't want; he only took them because I said we won't be getting any for a couple of months as you are going off sick for a bit".

One thing was clear; we had one of the security men in our pocket as we had dropped stuff off for his daughter and also for him, so I used him as much as I could. I took my brother down one Sunday and the first thing was to give him a signed St Helens shirt for his daughter. He was made up, then he said, "What are you doing down here?" and I said, "Our kid's oven is fucked so I was thinking, is it okay with you that we have a look for one?" and he said, "Yes, mate. You know where they are", so I drove my van into the building but away from the cameras. My brother was buzzing; he was like a child! He said, "Fuck me, how much stuff is in here, pal?" and I said, "About £800 million pounds", and he said, "Can we go anywhere on this fork truck?" and I said, "You can when I am driving!" so, I took him on a tour of the warehouse. We ended up putting all sorts in the van. We were looking for his cooker and this thing was 1200mm wide and three people couldn't lift it, so we looked all over the place then found one in the racks, so I got up with the forks and me and him pulled it over to the forks. He said, "Mate, I can't tell you how excited I am", and I said, "Get this in and have a look round", so he was all over the place - pots and pans, kettles and toasters, and he said, "Are we splitting this?" and I said, "No, mate. I can get mine anytime; this is yours", and he said, "I don't want to go home! This is amazing! No fucking wonder you work seven days a week - I would too if all this was here".

He was made up when we got home; he didn't shut up all the way home. He said, "I felt like a child with all that stuff". I reminded him that you could only take one of each or they would notice it was gone and he said, "Right. You're clever, mate, that's why you have got where you are!"

I was telling my mate who was working with me and he said, "Why don't you try with him on security when we get down next week?" so I went to see him and said, "Mate, do you mind if I get in early and sort me and my mate a cooker?" and he said, "Not at all, pal", so I put £100 in his pocket and said, "Get you and the wife a drink on me". So, next day, we changed vans and went up in the Merc long van, parked at the side and took out 10 range cookers and put some of them on their side just to get them in. Then I rang Rat Boy and said, "I will be with you in 20 minutes". We started to move stuff closer and waited for break time at 10.30 am and then loaded the van again. It was very hard work as both of us had bad backs and bad shoulders, but we did it. I took them to Rat Boy because my mate had started our work sheet. Then I called at the butty shop and got security a butty, and went round to my mate and we had ours. He said, "I am fucked", and I said, "Here, this will ease your pain", and gave him £2000. He said, "Right, that was well worth the pain. Are we going again?" and I said, "No, pal. Give it a couple of weeks and we will look then".

Then Monk said, "So are we splitting that?" and I said, "No, you take the £16,000 as you need it now and I will wait for the rest at the end of next week or the week after." So, Monk said, "Are you okay waiting?" and I said, "Yes, I am fine, don't worry. You just do what you have to and take my home number and ring me a couple of weeks after the stocktake as they will be phoning you about it when you're off", so he said, "Mate, that's so kind of you". I asked if he had enough money now and he said he did. He gave me a hug and said, "You are brill", and I said, "Right, get back on your truck and get me these items for my mates". So, he went off, loaded 8 items on and then brought a box of Bose DAB radios, 6 in the box, and said, "These are for you and your family". I thanked him then I drove to security, had a brew and said to him, "I will see you Thursday, pal". I dropped the box of radios at home then dropped off 4 cookers and 2 fridge freezers and everyone asked what they owed and I said, "Don't worry, I am glad I can help". That's why everyone loved me because I wouldn't charge anyone for anything I got and the only reason I took the money for dropping the stuff off is because it was to someone I didn't know. Plus, it was a friend of the lads in the warehouse, so I took the van back and there was a microwave and a set of pans for the bloke I had got the 7.5 ton wagon off and it was free, so I just got in my van and drove home.

The week after, when I went up to Blackburn, I rang Rat Boy and he said, "I haven't got all the money, but I should have it tomorrow. Leave it with me and I will see what I can sort. One guy owes us over £20k so I will get that and ring you later". So I went to the site, got my list done then went out with the manager for some dinner, which I paid for. We then went to the cake shop and he spent around £40 on cakes and I used my card. He said, "You don't have to buy everything", and I said, "I do because you're paying me for being away from the site." When we got in his car, I graced him £200, and he said, "Fuck me, thanks for that, pal. Send me 2 invoices; just keep both under £1000. Put down whatever you want. In fact, it's month end; send me 3 invoices!" I then went back to see Rat Boy and he gave me £54,000. I said, "You didn't have to give me cash; you could have transferred it into my bank," and he said, "Great, we will do that next time". I said, "Don't forget, do not take anything for a few weeks now because it is stocktake". We said goodbye and I went home, tried to fit the money into the safe and it wouldn't fit so I had to keep it in a drawer under my T-shirts. With all the work and all the cash, I had made over £200,000 in that month but only showed £72,000 through my books. I put receipts in for over £50,000 and put the cheque into my mate's old bank account. He had no access to it as I had the card and the cheque book, but every now and then, I would give him £1000 when we were out having a drink and he was made up with that. I told him to let me know if he ever needed anything for home. We had been friends for a long time and we trusted each other and would always be there for each other.

Each Christmas, I always tried to help someone out who had no money. A couple of times, I had helped my wife's friends but other times, I would help a young family who had nothing. I would ask the lads at rugby and they would bring the kids for training, or if it was for a big family, I would put £1000 in a Christmas card and take it to the house, knock and ask for Mum. I would say, "I have spoken to a couple of lads at the club, and you could do with this. Open it when I have gone". If they were smaller families, I would help two out, giving them £500 each, but I got satisfaction out of that because I was helping someone. Everyone in my local area only had good things to say about me. I even did jobs for people for free if they had no money. There were 3 local pensioners and I did all their work for free no matter what. I was just glad to help out, to see the smile and to get a hug off a sweet old lady was priceless. At Christmas, I would call with a card, a nice bottle of red wine and a box of chocolates for each one and it was lovely to give to them. Each one was very sweet and very grateful, but it was a love I didn't get as a child. These three older ladies I helped showed me the love that a mother should give and love that I was never given, but you do get used to it when you're younger.

I am hoping that the ex-wife will be giving our grandchildren some of the money she took from me. I never understood when she said it was <u>our</u> money, when it was me who worked and stole seven days a week and even paid for holidays for her parents. So, no, it wasn't our money; it was my saving that got me the money. She always said, "If you ever get caught, I don't want anything to do with you", but she had spent the money for 15 years. What she didn't realise was if the tax man came, which she threatened me with, that she would also go to prison too and I was so looking forward to her doing this because I knew she couldn't do jail. It wouldn't bother me as I had done Young Offenders, but it would have killed her. She would be an accessory to fraud as she even banked the cheques in her name, but there's still time; let's hope we both go because she will lose her home and everything she has purchased with the money. Fuck me, that would make my life, not my day, if she went to jail. A couple of years inside would do me good - I would be able to get some rest and you never know, I may learn a new skill! I have always been interested in forgery and computer fraud. I wish I was clever enough because I would be sat at that computer 16 hours a day, not taking off the working class, just hitting the big companies who like to rip us all off.

No matter what I had given my wife, she didn't care; she just wanted more, and she got everything she ever wanted – cars, watches, holidays and jewellery, but nothing seemed to be enough. Even when both kids left home, she was made up because she could have a big bedroom with an en suite well away from me. and she used to say she didn't like wakening me up when she got up at 5.30 am to go to work at 7.30 am, but she didn't give a fuck; she was only interested in what money I had made. We had booked another big holiday with her parents - this was the 5th one I had paid for - this came to £26,500 plus I gave them £1000 spending money and paid any extra bills in the hotel. We were away for two weeks and I was in agony; my back was killing me and I ended up running out of blood pressure tablets even though I knew I had packed a full strip that had 14 on it, so I tried at the chemist and they couldn't give me any, so we got on with the holiday, but I could only walk so far as it was in Vegas and it was a long walk and over 115 degrees. I had walked for around 4 hours and then said, "Right, I am getting the bus back to the hotel," and when I got back, I went back to the room and took my medication, had a shower and sat on the bed and put the tv on. When she came back, she wouldn't speak to me and wasn't interested that I was struggling with the heat and the pain.

When we were out for a meal one night, her dad asked me how I was and I said I needed my back sorting out when we got home. I said, "When I get back, I am going to book private to see someone and see what he says", then my loving wife said, "If you end up in a wheelchair, I AM NOT STAYING AROUND TO PUSH YOU IN A WHEELCHAIR !!" Her mum said, "That's awful that! How can you say that to your husband?" and she said, "I am just saying". When we got home, I just went about my work, but I knew I needed my back done and it was booked in for late September, but a week after we got home, she went away with her friends for 4 days and I gave her £600 spending money and her friends £120 to get a drink at the airport. She never phoned once while she was away and when she got back, she was a little stand-offish but I thought it was me so I just carried on working 7 days a week. About a week later, when I had finished work, she said, "Can I talk to you? I want out". I thought she wanted to leave work, but she said, "No, this; I want out of this. I think it's the end of us". I was dumbstruck! I didn't expect that, and she got in the car and drove off, then the next thing, her mum and dad came and sat with me saying, "Sorry, mate, I have tried to talk to her for the past couple of weeks". So, they knew everything and I knew nothing! Then, she came back home and said to me, "Do you want to tell the kids?" and I said, "No, do I fuck! It's your decision - you tell them!" So, I went upstairs and put the tv on. Don't get me wrong, I was upset, then the girls came, and I could hear them shouting, "What the fuck? You have everything!" They came to me and we all cried together, and I said, "Listen, don't worry; it will all be yesterday's news soon", and they left. I was dumbstruck. I could understand if I was a twat or if it was because I was out all the time, but I was the oversight - it was her who was a bitch, demanding all the time and going out with her mates. All I did was work and pay for everything, but then again, you could class me an idiot.

On the Tuesday night, she came into the back room and said, "Can you get a total off your investments so we can sort out money?" I reminded her that she had said she would never come for my money, but she said she needed it for a house. I spoke to one of the staff and got the total sent over. It showed I had around

£640,000 left after I had given the kids money for their homes and given her brother money and she said, "You have got more than that!" I told her that last month, I had taken out £100,000 and split it between the girls, so she said, "Well, I will take £300,000 of that and then the house", and I said, "You didn't put anything into the house! I bought it and I paid for all the work and paid all the bills!" She said, "That doesn't matter. My dad said the house must be worth £500,000 because of how much work you have done to it". After all I had done for them over the years; I was stunned, and I said, "Yes, all the work I have done, not you, because all you have done is lived a life of luxury, everything paid for by me while I work 7 days a week and you have never saved or paid a penny into the savings. It has been me since I was 18 years old. You were on £40,000 a year at work and I still gave you money. What the fuck did you do with your wages? I paid all the bills for the house - you even had a free car plus free insurance and my company card for fuel and you moaned when I had a go because you used my company card to buy clothes! My accountant went mad! How do I put through Dorothy Perkins on my building business? And not just the odd thing, it was hundreds! Why the fuck did you have no wages left? I wouldn't be able to spend your wages if I sat in the pub 7 days a week but you ran out on your third week. And, like a prick, I would give you £200-£300 to get you over." If I told people what she used to spend in a month on clothes and shoes and coats and shite, they wouldn't believe me. If she wanted something expensive, she would say, "Should we go to the Trafford Centre for a ride?" and it was a ride into Selfridges and she would say, "That's lovely", and like a prick, I would get it for her; that was the only reason I was in that shop. She didn't want me to go, she just wanted me to spend my money. She was very clever; too clever for me, but I was too soft.

So, we signed an amicable agreement that when I paid her the money, she would leave me alone. Then, the day after, she got a letter from my solicitor for a divorce. I told him to put it down to me, as long as it was done asap. When she said she was amazed that I had filed for divorce so quickly, I told her that we may as well get it over and done with then she could move on with whoever. I just wanted her out of the house. I even got her stuff for her house from work; a fridge freezer, microwave, kettle, toaster, plates, bowls and a few other things. I know it sounds stupid but I have given everything away all my life so I couldn't leave her out, even with what she had done to me. and the day she moved out, I said I would stay out of the house and she could text when she was done, so she tested about 5 pm saying they were behind so I went to my mate's. After a while, my phone went, and it said 'all done you can come back home now'.

That was it, so I told my mate, "Thanks. I am going home". He asked if I would be okay and said that he would always be there for me and I said, "Yes, mate. I know and I appreciate it". Then I drove home. When I drove down the drive, the house was in darkness, so I went in and put some lights on. I closed the blinds and walked around putting lights on. It was strange; something had changed. I was going to be on my own all the time now and it didn't feel nice. I didn't drink but I did go over the road to the pub for a pint, but that didn't make me feel any better. I felt empty. I was very upset but not because she had gone, it was the way it was done and what money she took because she knew I had no pension and I wanted to keep some money back for when I finished work. She went mad when I paid out for the kids' homes and the gardens. I ended up spending close to a million pounds and I gave a lot of money to her brother when he was sick, and I wasn't bothered about money. I always told her I would get that back over a million in less than a year but she just didn't want me to spend anything. Then I got told she had been planning on moving out since April that year so 6 months before she told me, but she had been photocopying all my investment documents and that really pissed me off. I don't know how it didn't break me. My head was all over the place because I couldn't understand how she could do this to me after all I had done for her and her family. It was horrible.

My old team used to have 'past player' events every Christmas and between then and New Year, everyone got together. The problem was no matter if I went to any 'past players', the lads could recall loads of stuff that happened in some of the games we all played in, but I don't remember 99% of my playing time so I can't really put much down about it. I would have liked to as I spent 9 years at one club and that is a lot of games to play at one club and a lot of friends to make on the way. I also played for 2 years at a pro club, but my mind is blank, so sorry, I would love to tell you some of the stuff we did on the pitch but I would need a lot of the players' input to help me write it down. I know we got into some bad things off the pitch after the game while drinking on the coach but as I was always told, we had a great time, so even though I can't remember them myself, at least most of my old playing mates can look back and say they had a good time.

I also had my back operation cancelled until the year after, so I thought it was fine because I was still working and me and my mate were still going in and loading 10 into the Merc Sprinter and I would give him £1000 and he was made up. I ended up with £5000 so it was a good day, and we were doing it twice a

Week. No one on site had a clue because the Monk had left, so we just got in before everyone else and got loaded. I would do the drop, pick some food up and if we could, bang in another load. Sometimes, we only got 6 or 8 in but that was enough for a second run and it was helping me to build my money up again. It was like a game - get what you can to get yourself back on track. I knew I didn't have long left and was still earning good money from working, but also good money off Monk and I needed to build myself a bit of a nest egg after losing so much money to my ex-wife, so I put as much effort in as I could and started to load my safe up again. I needed to keep everything away from the banks so she couldn't come back.

I was on a very good run and then I was working on a job 13 feet up a ladder and the ladder went backwards, and I landed on the concrete, breaking the bone in my spine, and shattered my right wrist, so then I had to have blue plaster fitted so I could go into work and the blue went with my jumper and I put a latex glove on to hide it. The next problem was I was told to go on the roof at work and this was a huge no because they had their own roofer. Anyway, they couldn't get him, and I was told 'go up or don't come back' so I had no option. As I got to the top, all the duck boards were rotted so I got to the job and took out the broken glass and just left it in the roof ridge. Then I made my way back. I had to walk around 40 metres on wet, crumbling duck boards and, as I got 10 metres from the end to the roof ladder, the duck boards snapped, and I slid down the asbestos roof. I ripped all my left arm open, and if I would have gone through the roof, the oven was below so that would have been it for me, so I had to report what had happened and the guy who gave me my work stopped giving me work because I reported it. However, I had no option as someone saw me from below and I was bleeding badly from my left arm. Due to this and the fact that it was not my job to do, I ended up losing my contract, but I still carried on going to Bury and Blackburn to meet Monk on a night or early in the morning at 4 am. My mate said it was probably the best thing to happen because I would have ended up getting caught in the end. They had been investigating the losses for three years, so maybe he was right.

We were asked to do an emergency office knock-through as the accounts department needed a bigger office, so I checked it all out and asked when they wanted this done. said the boss said, "If you go and sit in that office and can get me a price, you can start tonight". It was already 2 pm on a Friday so I went into the office and one of the managers came in. I told him I was a bit lost as to what was needed. Did they want new carpets and blinds? He said, "Forget the carpet and blinds, just get rid of the electrics and make sure the wall was not supporting anything". I told him it wasn't, so he said, "Well, one has been put in for the electrics but don't forget to charge to make safe the electrics and you have to make good the false ceilings. I would go in at around £18,000 but there is room on that for extras too". So, I gave in my cost as a rough rushed estimate, and we started at 5 pm. I brought two of the brickies in and it took them 30 minutes to take down the wall then load it out of the second floor into a skip lifted up by a fork truck, so we had everything out for 7.30 and the room cleaned and hoovered for 8.30 pm. We just left my tools to do the plastering and electrics the next day and I paid the 2 brickies £140 each so they were made up. I stopped at security and the young lad was on. I said, "Here, pal," and gave him £20 and said, "Book me out at 1am", and we went to the pub. I only had a soft drink then home to get ready for the day after. Nest day, I made good all the plasterwork and the floors and tied in the ceilings, then I covered the ceiling joint with a 150mm plastic bead done with double-sided tape and sealed with cork for extra support. Then we had a good deep clean of what was now one big office so all the carpets, desks, chairs and cabinets looked spotless. We got done at 1 pm so we went to watch our local rugby side and I said, "We will go in tomorrow, mate, because they will think it took all weekend". It still needed painting and a second good clean to make sure, then we spent over 2 hours going through the offices as they had loads of stuff, all brand new in boxes – radios, kettles, hoovers, big boxes of good pens with a USB stick on it, the metal cups for keeping tea warm - it was like Supermarket Sweep! When we had filled our boots on the way out, I gave security £20 for a drink and said, "Book me out at 6 pm when you leave, please", and he said, "No problem". Then we went back the next day and walked through the offices just picking whatever you needed. There was all sorts there, so my mate was made up; new leather chair for his computer, I took some desk down and one of the lads had asked for some for his office so we dropped him 3 off with drawers on rollers and some filling cabinets and a couple of cupboards. He said, "What do I owe you, Tuck?" I said, "You're fine; get me a pint next time". We got back to site and the electricians had come in and they just put a dado rail round with sockets on, but they were shit and we walked off as I said I was not helping because I had priced the electrics and didn't get it anyway. We were asked to move out the furniture and bring the new stuff in and set it up, so we got another two days added to the original job, but the electricians had made a mess and left the job. In the office were two women directors and they were not happy. The manager rang me and asked if I was still on site. I said, "Yes, mate". He said, "Can you nip back to that job?" When we got there, the two directors went mad. One said, "These two lads have worked through the night Friday and Saturday and even came in on Sunday to clean. They did an amazing job, but now look at the state of the place! It was spotless this morning when we came in!" I said, "It's okay, we will sort it out for you". So, we had to do a big clean again and we were still there at 6. I went downstairs and got two vases as someone had left a bunch of flowers under the stairs, so I cleaned them, put water in and put one on each desk and left a post-it note saying, 'hope this is okay for you'. Next day, they were buzzing! They absolutely loved us and couldn't thank us enough and all it took was a bunch of flowers that was going into the bin and two vases from the big office. I ended up with an estimate for over £18,000 and got another £4000 on it for extras, so came out with a good pay day and on the weekend, I was doing floor repairs inside and took over £7000 plus VAT for the floor repairs the lads had done at the weekend on top, so again, it was another huge earner for the weekend.

The main man I used to get my work off was leaving for another company and it left just one more who I could manipulate a bit, but then they took this guy on and fuck me, what he didn't know wasn't worth knowing! But when it came to doing the job, he didn't have a fucking clue! This bloke had somehow blagged his way into a good job but I used to just go along with what he said and believe me, you could not buy this man in any way at all. So, everything had to be done above board when you did any work for him. The other guy was okay and we used to laugh and take the piss when we were on our own in a meeting and when I was giving him his envelope. Soon after that, the new man wanted to be in every meeting and he decided what could or couldn't be done, so I thought, 'Sound, I will not give you any information'. I asked him for a work schedule so the lads could work to it. I was still doing my stuff at the other sites but this new bloke started to visit the other sites I don't know why but I just stuck to the rules.

Then he asked me to do a large concreting job. Now, I had done thousands, so I said, "Can you give me the schedule and the details of the excavation, the reinforcement size and the type of concrete mix, please, so I can price the concrete?" Then he said, "Concrete is concrete". I said, "No, there are many different types; you can get a C30, a C40, a C50, or a C60 and can you tell me what slump you require?" He said, "What do you mean, slump?" I said, "A concrete slump determines how much water is added to the mixture." So, he said, "Well, what do you normally use?" and I said, "It depends on where it is going. If it is on the road, a C60 medium slump; if it's on a footpath, C30-35 medium to wet slump. Have a read and let me know what you want". Now, I knew this was pissing him off but he was a fucking arsehole. So, he sent back '150mm deep 8mm reinforcing with a C40 mix medium slump' so I sent an email back and copied the other bloke I paid and their big boss on it, then wrote, "After looking at your email and request for the concrete to be a C40 at 150mm deep with 8mm reinforcing, this would not be adequate for this area due to the heavy traffic i.e. 20-ton fork truck. This would crumble like a biscuit. I would recommend that the excavation is around 300mm with 100mm of hardcore vibrate-plated down with 12mm reinforcing and a minimum of a C50 medium slump to be laid; this will work out more expensive but it is better to install the adequate materials."

Anyway, this really pissed him off and he requested a meeting and, in the meeting, he said, "All you had to do was phone me", and I said, "You told me off last week for doing a job and not letting you know about it before it was done, so we agreed that all work to be carried out would be emailed first." He had no answer to that and then went back to the concreting job and said, "Can you price both the original one I sent and the one you sent back?" I said, "The first thing is, I am not interested in pricing the one you sent me because it will not work and my reputation is on each job I do, but I will price you for the second one that I sent over". A couple of days later, the other boss said, "Listen, he has got another price off the company that did the work in Chester", and I said, "The one where all the concrete broke up?" and he said, "Yes". I asked him to let me know what is the price was. A couple of days after, this prick rang and said, "Are you on site at Blackburn?" and I said, "Yes". He asked me to meet him so I went along and he said, "Have you done the estimate for the concrete?" I said, "Nearly; just waiting for the steel price". He said he needed it today so I said I would send it over later. I got outside and rang the other boss and he told me the other price was £32,000, so I went home and sent a price for £38,500. The next day, my boss friend said, "You have gone way over", and I said, "I know. I don't want it; the job is a twat to get to and I would sooner let them fuck it up, to be honest".

So, then the guy got me in and said, "You are way over our other estimate. Would you like to drop your price?" and I said, "No". He said, "I am giving you the chance of a big job here," and I said, "To do it right, that is what it is going to cost". So, they got other company in and I was still doing another job on site, but it was like a fun show. They turned up with 3 men in a car, no tools, no floor breakers, no dumper and no fucking idea. I was then asked to go for a meeting and he asked if I would be willing to go and help with the other company to get the job started. I said, "No, because it is a conflict of interest and I do not wish for my men to be held responsible for anything that another company is doing". said he then said, "Why are you being so awkward?" So, I told him, "You have selected your contractor and if they are unsure what they are doing, they should not be here". He said, "You know what, I thought you would help out". I said, "Are you listening to what you're saying? You want me to go and mother some shite company you have got in because they don't know what to do!" and then I stood up and said, "Oh, by the way, all three are sat in the car on site smoking weed and I am sure it is against the rules. Also, you're not allowed to have your car inside. They are eating their chips at dinner time at the job location when food is not allowed on site; you have to use the canteen, so please try to do your own job", and I walked out.

I went back to the lads and carried on with my work and then the other boss, who was my friend, came over and said, "Mate, will you come and have a look at what they are doing and make sure it is safe and it is right?" When we got there, they were drilling the concrete close to the wall and the bricks at the bottom were coming loose, so I said to the boss, "They need to put a saw line through the concrete at least 12 inches in from the wall". He asked why and I said, "The wall is built on that concrete; if they don't, the wall will fall down", so I left him to sort that out.

After that, I had started to go into work and when I was in meetings, I stopped taking shit and abuse off the company boss I didn't like. I don't know why but I started to tell him he was wrong and he had no idea about the building and to be truthful, he didn't, he was just a knob head. Some of the times he would say to me, "It is my choice who gets the work", and one day, in a bigger meeting with about 8 people, I said, "You are a fucking prick! You have no idea about the building trade or the electrical trade. You are full of shit. You may bullshit your way through the job, but if it wasn't for me telling you what to say, you would have been out on your arse 8 months ago. You come up with ideas that can't be done then let someone else sort it out and when it's done right, you get the credit for it; that's wrong!" and I walked off, got in the van and went home.

After that, I carried on doing what work was given to me and I went on filling my van and getting whatever I could, because this twat had dropped my work down because we didn't get on. So, I got to site every time it was possible and filled my van because I wanted to get my account filled again before things ended. I could see them stopping my work because I couldn't get on with this twat – he had no idea at all.

I had hit the point in my life again where my jeans were tight. To be truthful, all I had ever done was wear work clothes; I never put jeans on because I was always at work, and when I got home, I would wear shorts and a vest, so I did a couple of men's shops; some were harder than others, but I like the challenge. I even went back with some T-shirts I had bought on eBay and swapped them, along with 8 pairs of tracksuit bottoms. I was getting the bottoms off eBay for £5 to £10 and changing them for the new Adidas £120 ones and as a sports shop, you would think they would pull you first time, but they were too wrapped up in chatting crap to each other, so I just went with it.

My mate though I was nuts, but it was something built into me; I couldn't help myself. Even getting my shopping - that self-scan is like a dream! Just get to the till and tell the woman there is someone down the aisle and he put something in his coat, and she is off like a shot with the security man so nice clear path.

Even time for you to pack your bags and just leave the self-scan on the table. I had got friendly with the security man in Blackburn, and I rang him and said my cooker had broken and was it okay to call that Saturday night to find a replacement? He said, "No problem", so I went to get my mate at 7.30 pm. He said, "What you doing? England is playing!" and I said, "So are we. Come on!" We got there and went into chat to him. I gave him £200, and he said, "What's that for?" and I said, "My cooker is worth £800". I told him it would take us a bit to find one, so we drove round and then we just went over to the Rangemasters and loaded 10, all on their side, as that was the only way to get 10 in the van. Then we went back round and I said, "I got one but it's not the same, but it will do", and he offered the money back and I said, "Don't be silly, mate, thank you". We had also loaded in 10 microwaves, a couple of boxes of kettles and toasters and a wine cooler for my mate, then we had to meet the Rat at his unit and offload and I gave him a couple of microwaves. He gave me £8000 cash, so I gave my mate £2000, and he got his wine coolers and some other bits for him and his family. He said, "Are you sure, mate? This is a lot of money", and I said, "I can't do it on my own, pal, so don't worry about it; see you in work tomorrow".

I was asked about my rugby days by a guy I met online. He was acting for all the rugby union players with memory loss and to be truthful, I don't remember any of the games I played in. I remember something like ten seconds of a game but if I go to a 'past players', I don't even remember the players' names and I do get a little embarrassed about it, so I took this guy on and had a brain scan in King's College Hospital, this very strong scanner in London, and then to see a psychiatrist after, so I got the train there and a taxi to the hospital. It killed me because my back was in bits, so I got in the scanner and it took about ten minutes to get me laid flat on my back and then, when I got comfy, I just wanted to go to sleep, but this scanner was so strong that your teeth shook and felt like they were coming out. Also, your tattoos got warm, and it was loud. I was in it for 90 minutes and then had to go to another part to see the psycho lady and draw things, build with blocks and then join dots up but I was in there around 90 minutes and she was asking me stuff I had no idea about, but I tried. Then, at the end, she said, "You did a drawing on a pink piece of paper when you first came in. Can you draw it again?" and I said, "Are you sure you gave me a piece of paper because I do not remember you giving me a pink piece of paper". She said, "Try to think", so I just got the paper and drew a square on it and said, "Here, I have no idea what I am doing", and she said, "Okay, let's wrap up". Then I got a taxi back to the station and a train home. I left at 10 am and got home at 11.35 pm, took my night-time painkillers and sleeping tablets, had a shower and got into bed. I needed it done because my memory is shocking, and I keep forgetting words.

I didn't hear anything for around 4-5 weeks, then in the last week in March, my doctor rang me at 6.20 pm. I get on great with him. He said, "How come you didn't tell me you were going to London for this scan to be done?" and I said, "I didn't think it would make any difference, Doc," and he said, "I have got some of your results back but not them all, and it shows you have a large mass on the front left lobe of your brain". I asked him what that meant and he said, "Don't worry, I have asked for the rest of the results, the prognosis, the diagnosis and the treatment, but I want you to go and get all your bloods done tomorrow.

Let's get them done and when we get the rest of the results, we will send you to Walton or Clatterbridge for another brain scan". I was gobsmacked and said, "Will I be ok?" and he said, "Don't worry, let's get the results and get our own investigation started, then we are in front". So, I sat down and cried for a bit. I couldn't sleep that night; my mind was all over the place. I thought, 'This can't be happening to me; fuck me, what have I done wrong?' I didn't tell my girls, I only told my best friend and work partner but now I have planned for both results, good or bad, but I know I will have to tell my girls soon. I would like to know what is going to happen to me before I tell the kids and let them start to panic, and I know they will, because my close friend and brother-in-law had a brain tumour. He was only 42 years old, an absolutely wonderful bloke. I would hate to go the same way as he went because he was in pain all the time but didn't like to show it. He was a legend top rugby player, very highly respected in the game and loved by a lot of people, a dream friend to have, and I miss him loads and think about him most days. Everyone loved him; there were over 2000 at his funeral and it killed me when he passed away. Nothing seemed to be the same after losing him; he was the most positive person I have ever met and loved by thousands of people throughout the town and throughout the rugby league and I really do miss him.

In all the time I knew him, he never once said to me, "I don't like that person" because he wasn't like that. He was kind and funny and only saw the best in people. One day, he even said to me, "I don't know why you married my sister; she is a bossy bitch!" and that was her brother. But to be truthful, he was right; she was a bossy bitch and she wasn't a nice person. She always wanted something and I would just get it to keep her happy, but then she would want something else - you just can't win.

I do know one thing; I cannot go the same way as he did because he hid his pain, so I will decide when I go. First things first, I have to get the girls round and tell them, but not all of it. I will try and see how that goes; as long as they understand and I can tell them not to worry, I can get things done. If the results are good, we can carry on doing what I was doing, but if they are bad, it will all change. I will sell my home within two weeks, rent a small place and give the money from my home to the people around me who have got fuck all and who have been there for me. Whatever is left will go to the grandkids. Both my girls have had enough - they can look after themselves now they are settled down, have nice homes and their own family, but yet again, it was me who gave them the money, me who renovated their homes, me who paid for the gardens to be made over and me who gave them the money to buy the items in the house. Please note - FUCK ALL OFF THEIR MUM!

After getting the results from my brain scan, they say it is now a lesion, and in May 2021, I found out that back in July 2014, I was sent for a brain scan because I couldn't get rid of my headache and the Neurosurgeon has said, "We have looked at the scan he had in May 2014 and the lesion is only slightly bigger", so my question is, why the fuck didn't you tell me in May 2014 that I had a Brain Lesion? Because after reading up about what this is, it answers a lot of questions I have had over the years - why my eyesight is blurred, why I get involuntary movements of my arms and hands, why my mood has changed, why I have become more aggressive, why I can't be arsed doing anything, what made me not want to go the gym to see the lads, why can't I remember anything about my past as everything I have written is taken out of my diaries, why have I got tinnitus, why can't I remember any people's names, why can't I remember any of my rugby career and why do I keep getting a pulsing sound in my head? It's like when pregnant women have that thing put on to listen to the baby's heart. A lot of things have changed in my life since 2010-2012. I was always mad at work with the lads. I would go off at the slightest thing and I would throw my phone at the wall if my delivery was late and yes, I had to replace the phone, but I didn't care because I had the key to the main office and at the back of the office was a big cupboard and yes, it was full of mobile phones. So, I had gone from back when they had the Nokia through to the Apple Phone. There were hundreds of mobiles in there and I got phones for my wife and kids and I have 6 spares at home just in case, and when the new phones would come out like the Apple iPhone 8 up to the iPhone X, I used to change mine all the time. The funny thing was, the lady in the office rang me and asked me to go up. She was great with me and said, "Can you do me a favour? Can you change the lock on this cupboard? I think the cleaners are going in." So I said, "Why? What do you keep in there?" and she said, "The works phones", and she opened the door and I said, "I know who to see if I need a new phone!" So, she said, "Sort the lock and I will sort you one out". So, I took the lock out of the door and took it to my mate's shop and said, "Match that, pal", and he gave me the same one, so after he had cut me a key, I had a brew with him and took the lock back, but before I took the lock up to her office, I taped the box shut with a bit of tape. I went in and she said, "I can't thank you enough. How many keys are there?" and I said, "I will tell you when I open the box." So, I opened it in front of her and said, "There are three", so I changed the lock over and gave her the three keys, leaving me with a spare in my van for my next hit. She offered me an iPhone and I said, "No, thank you, I hate Apple phones. I just like the Nokia, but thank you for the offer though", and she said, "If we get any new Nokias in, I will let you know". I walked away leaving her with that thought that if any more phones go, it can't be him because he doesn't like iPhone!

 I have had a great life up to now. I didn't get the best wife; I fucked up there, but I have got two lovely girls and three stunning grandkids. Yes, my wife left and took everything I had, but I am not a money person. I don't care for money but I do care that I have lost my company and my wife due to my ill health. I did suffer with depression again and I will tell you, everyone I had looked after all the time I had my company disappeared, plus, I ended up losing the good contacts I had on all the sites and also lost the money my company was earning each year, between £700,000 to £900,000, but I had to get past it and stop thinking of the past. At least I have my home, which is mortgage-free and my children have been given the best start in life. They are happy so I think my job is done. Don't get me wrong; I wish I didn't have to have my back done because I would still be earning a lot of money, but like my mate said, "II think we had a very good run", and he is right because I always say you get greedy, you get caught. I was never greedy - I only did it when I was asked by Monk, but in the end, Monk ended up leaving so that would have put a stop to it then. I never asked him to get stuff to sell; it was him who saw the money and wanted more. That's what happens - you get money, you want more and the more you get, the more you want. I did take a huge lot of items, I would say over 100,000, for my friends and family but I was told if I needed anything just help yourself, so I did it in the right way. Sometimes they would offer me stuff that had just come in and I used to say, "Thank you, but I don't need it and none of my family have asked for anything". Doing this kept them off my track because if you take everything they offer, you will look bad, so the best thing is politely saying thanks, but no thanks. Even if you do need it, refuse and then just take one out of stock because they won't think of you because you have refused the one they offered you. It's all mind games, but that's the best way to get people to trust you. If I was desperate, I used to buy things at the staff shop so they could see I was buying stuff. I even had my own key for the staff shop but I didn't kill it. If someone got something for me, I always treated him and walked away.

Now I am back to my old self, I don't think I will change my ways, but I have about £900 in the bank, and I have my house, but it doesn't bother me at all. I've done what I wanted in life. I wanted to be a millionaire and I made it to 3.4 million, then all I did was give it away. Yes, I did give some to the wrong people; you do make mistakes, but I made sure my kids were looked after and my ex-wife definitely ended up coming out on top even though she saved fuck all, but you have to get past that and carry on. When I sit and think about it, yes, I am back where I started when I was 20 years old, but I own a nice house and car. I may only have a little bit of money but I don't drink and don't smoke so I only spend money on house bills and food. I would love to get a little bit fitter and start the gym, but I can't; my full body is fucked. I have had a disc taken out of my spine through my throat, both shoulders reconstructed twice and now need a new ball and socket to my left shoulder. I have had my right wrist reconstructed, two big hernias fixed that still kill, ripped half my quad on my left leg and bled that much my body went black from my belly button to my knees. I've had a small tear in my right quad, broke every finger on both hands, had my left knee cleaned out and then had metal work fitted to my lower spine, and to top it off, they find a mass on the front left lobe of my brain. I take loads of painkillers, even 50mg morphine with the rest of them and 7 sleeping tablets, but apart from the pain and all the injuries, I am back at the beginning if you're looking at my money situation, and to be totally honest, I don't care. I can't say I am happy because I am not, but only because of the way things were done.

I am taking antidepressants so I can't be happy, but I hope someday I will get off them and someday, I will be able to lower my morphine and other painkillers so I can go over the road and have a pint because I haven't had a pint for years and that was at a wedding. It was 13 years ago when I stopped going to the pub because I used to go to work at 4 am and didn't want to lose my driving licence. If I had, I would have lost my contract and a lot of money and that was the main time to load up.

I can look back and tell you that if I had kept on going out on Friday, Saturday and Sunday, there is no way I could have done what I managed to do. I did lose a lot of friends by stopping going out - they called me a miserable twat - but I think I made the right choice. I was more focused on making money and I did what I set out to do, even though I worked through the night, which was very profitable.

But now, looking back, I am grateful for the work they gave me and the life they provided for me and my family, but like my best mate said, I got out while I was ahead. I could have been caught and lost everything I had worked for and sat behind bars for a long time. I have had a great life and looked after a lot of people along the way, even some people I didn't know, but I enjoyed giving to people; that always makes me happy knowing I have made someone's day. Although 90% of the things I have given to people haven't cost me anything, the other 10% have cost me a lot of money but I got much more in return.

My advice to the younger people starting a company is this: it doesn't matter what the company does, the rules are still the same and you need to read along and keep this in your mind. This will work if you're trying to work your way up the ladder in a job too. This part is mainly for subcontractors on sites and sites that have things some of us would like at home - I would say we don't jump in headfirst; if you want to take something you have seen on site, leave it and keep your eye on it for a couple of days. Even if you move it to another location, leave it on site until at least a couple of weeks. If it stays in that location, move it to a different location for one day. If it's still there, then your safe to clear the space as it is known. Always get in with security first; give them cold drinks on hot days, drop them cakes off, drop them pies off, then offer to buy their breakfast so you can sit in the security hut and look at the cameras. Talk to him about whatever he wants to talk about; doesn't matter if it's soaps or musical theatre, just go along with it and start to make a bond; you need first name terms. Then, when you do have your brew in there, keep talking and study the cameras while you're doing it and if you are not sure about a camera, just walk over and look at it and he will ask you. "What's up?" Then you say, "I am sure I have just seen a fox pass that camera," and he will go on the camera and move it so you can work out where it is covering. Every place has a blind spot; even in Harrods there is a blind spot, but it is up to you to find it. Just study the cameras and work it out. It took me three years to find mine, but most of the time, we don't need it. Just be polite and take in cakes and stuff for staff in the office. That way, you soon gain respect because everyone talks about you. Make sure your work is good and clean, even staying late to get things done; that does impress people, just as long as where you are working is ready for the next day when they come into work, when it's clean they love it. Normally, you will be allocated a person or persons who ring you and ask you to price up the work on the site, so find out what they like, and if it's football or rugby, doesn't matter what team he supports, just get 4-6 tickets and on the Monday, put them in his drawer or inside an estimate and put a post-it note on it saying, "Just been given these by my suppliers but I don't like the game. Can you use them or give them to one of your friends to use so they don't go to waste?" If that person uses them, you are halfway there. Leave it a few more weeks then get 4 more and do the same; see if he uses them. If he does, great, you're 90% there. On your next one, when you sort the tickets, just put them in an envelope with £50 and a note saying, "Get your mates a drink on me". Now, if he comes back Monday and offers you it back, just say, "Honest, you keep it as I have given my accountant a receipt for the money on an invoice from the local tool shop. My mate did me one, so don't worry". If he takes it, you are there, then, because he has accepted money from you, so you can push for what you want. Try having a coffee with him and just ask if anyone else is pricing for the next job. If he says yes, just say, "Do you mind helping me out on price? I have no work for the lads after this week". Then, if he says yes, just say, "Thank you so much". Do not offer anything until he tells you what price you are up against. To give you an example, I was doing a job and my price was £22,000 and he said there was another company pricing for it. I hung on until everyone else had gone home and he was waiting and when he passed, I said, "Did you manage to sort that, pal?" All he had to do was tell me a rough price, but he gave me the estimate, so as soon as I went home, I wrote up a price including everything they had missed and set it in. Also, I had ordered some extra stuff to fit around the corner of the original job. Around two hours later, his boss rang me and asked to meet in his office and asked about the extra stuff I had put on, so I said, "Last time we were there, I spotted about 30 metres that was damaged and needed changing so I thought you would be better doing it with this job as the more you buy, the cheaper it is." He was so impressed that he gave me the job. Once I was finished, I gave him £3000 in an envelope and left it in his drawer. When he questioned me about it, I said, "You made me a lot of money on this job, so I owe you big time".

You will work at some sites and there will be women bosses. Remember, these are a different breed. Just keep saying, yes, miss, no problem, miss, and get it down as soon as possible and if anything is broken in her office, a shelf or a drawer or even a picture to go on the wall, just do it for free while you are there and make sure it is spotless when you leave. Call in the day after, knock on the door and ask is everything is okay. If she says yes, tell her what other bits you have done and it goes a long way. On your next visit, ask if she had a nice weekend and what she got up to. She will tell you something, and then say, "Do you like any sport? Do you ever go to any concerts?" If she says, "Yes, we went to watch some well-known singer at Manchester", ask her how it was, look interested and say, "I may take my girls to see (Name the Band) next month", and she may say, "Oh, we are going to see (This Person) the month after." Then say, "Do you go with your partner or friends?" Never say husband in case she is divorced or lesbian. MY LAST ONE WAS. Once you have the information, go and find tickets. Even if there is 10 of them, buy them, go into her office and play the same game. She may say, "I can't take these!" so just say "I thought of you when the group came up in conversation, so I said 'my boss is thinking of going. Can you sort her and her friends some tickets?' and he said not a problem. I asked for 10. I don't like the group so give them to your friends to use."

I would say 95% of the time she will say, "That is so kind of you!" Just say, "It's fine; if I can get you tickets free, it's the least I can do because you look after me at work and it's just a little thank you", but you need to stretch it out on a woman. I would just stick to the tickets for a good few months then say if she needs anything done at home, just let you know. As soon as you have done your first job, when she offers to pay, just say, "No, it's cost me nothing as I claim the materials through work and all it cost was a bit of my time - the least I could do!" and make sure the place is spotless and get your arse out.

So, the old saying is that you don't give to receive. Now this is true, but when you can strike a relationship up like I had at 8 different sites, and sometimes I was putting out £10,000 to a number of managers, I am sure it would work no matter where you are. Just be careful and go slow at the start and take it from me, you will know within the first few months who will take and who definitely not to offer anything to apart from a coffee and a cake. When you look at what I did, I made my goal and when I did, I was just the same person. Everyone liked me; I helped out whoever I could and I always gave people items for free. I was a hero to them but I must admit, it I got more pleasure helping people out. I was the person who walked into a pub and said, "Can I have a bottle of Bud and a brandy and have one yourself and get the drinks for everyone!" It seems strange and some may think that's big-headed, but you need to understand how many people know me; it is a lot, and they all know I was kind and helpful and what's £60 when you have a pub full of people with nothing but admiration for you and all those people thanking you? It's not a good feeling - it's an amazing feeling! And that's why, most of the time, I would do it again.

The last thing I will tell you is very true; you may have hundreds or thousands of friends like I had, but truthfully, you can count your close friends on one hand; think about it!

You can buy a watch for £20 or you can buy a watch for £85,000.00 but they both tell you the same time.

www.ingramcontent.com/pod-product-compliance
Lightning Source LLC
Chambersburg PA
CBHW030907080526
44589CB00010B/192